SITES OF MYSTERY & IMAGINATION

SITES OF MYSTERY & IMAGINATION

CHARLES WALKER

CHANCELLOR
PRESS

Cover photograph: © Matthew Weinberg / The Image Bank

First published in 1990 by The Hamlyn Publishing Group Limited

This 1998 edition published by Chancellor Press
an imprint of Reed Consumer Books Limited
Michelin House, 81 Fulham Road, London SW3 6RB

ISBN 0 75370 043 3

A CIP catalogue record for this book is available
at the British Library

Printed and bound in China

Produced by Toppan Printing Co., (H.K.) Ltd

Contents

Introduction

THIS book has been designed as a starting point for a study of arcane and occult sites in Europe: the text presupposes no special knowledge of the magical sciences, but offers a brief introduction to them, describing those aspects of occultism which are of special importance to the main European arcane centres. The book is intended both as a preparation for a unique European journey, and as an encouragement to anyone who wishes to make his own personal discovery of arcane lore.

It is hoped that after reading this book the reader will visit the mystery sites of Europe with confidence. As his knowledge grows, he will soon find himself able to build up his own personal repertoire of arcane places, which guide the perceptive visitor to a deeper comprehension of the spiritual nature of the world. Such a person would be among the most fortunate of all travellers, for he would have discovered the magic power which brings every place to life, and which reveals its own story of lost or hidden wonders. He will see with astonishment how Europe is filled with remnants of an arcane power.

The journey through Europe in search of lost secrets will lead to many unexpected discoveries. For example, there are zodiacs and astrological symbols in churches and cathedrals, curious relics of a dark art which was surely contrary to the tenets of the church. The façades of these buildings are occult books in stone, filled with demonic gargoyles, arcane symbols and alchemical devices. The prevalence and continuity of astrological symbolism is suprising – it stretches almost uninterruptedly from its emergence, in the eleventh century, to the twentieth-century astrological clocks of Worms and London.

For historical reasons certain areas in Europe contain distinctly different forms of arcane lore. The rocks at Externsteine, for example, are undoubtedly a telluric centre, the meeting point of terrestrial and subterranean currents, orientations and leys, while southwest France has its own special history of religious dissent, where there are still many castles which once harboured the Cathars and the Templars. Some parts of Germany are still linked with the dark days of medieval witchcraft through the survival of castles and old houses, while Brocken in the Harz mountains is indelibly stamped with the demonic seal of Goethe's Mephistopheles. Northern Italy has its unique collection of zodiacal calendars, and the country as a whole is steeped in arcane lore.

The oldest of the surviving centres of mystery are, of course, the prehistoric stone circles and alignments of which there are many in Britain and northern France. Intensive academic research into the meanings of these circles is still in progress, but it is clear that the most important circles, those at Callanish in Scotland, for example, and the vast complexes of Avebury and Stonehenge in the south of England were designed, among other things, as devices for recording and predicting solar and lunar phenomena.

The early forms of Christianity were soaked in a esoteric lore linked with the old mystery wisdom, and we see traces of this in many surviving symbols and images. In particular we can see how the European cathedral builders made use of stellar orientations, the fall of the sun's rays on certain symbols, the ancient mazes (or dancing circles, as some maintain) and a whole welter of arcane and astrological systems, most of which were derived from Arabic lore in the tenth and eleventh centuries. The strain of esoteric Christian symbolism, which may be traced with such dramatic effect in such churches as San Miniato al Monte, in Florence, or in Chartres cathedral, in France, is perhaps the most accessible of all arcane systems in Europe. The main problem is that some knowledge of medieval occult lore is needed in order to read the language of zodiacal and alchemical symbolism found in so many medieval cathedrals.

Alongside the development of esoteric Christianity, there grew strains of heresy, usually carefully hidden in the activities of secret societies, some of which were suppressed by the early church. Among the surviving systems which have left their symbols and artefacts in modern Europe are the complex cosmic notions of the Gnostics, the sacred bull-symbolism of the Mithraic centres, and the dualism of the Manichees, which flowered in the heretical movements of southern France, during the thirteenth and fourteenth centuries. The heretical Cathar villages and towns such as Albi, Carcassonne and Montségur have become places of pilgrimage in modern times for those who feel a kinship with the men and women who rejected much of the ritual and beliefs of the contemporary Catholic church.

Nominally, at least, the bloodthirsty suppression of the Cathars by the papacy put an end to their heresy, yet it left behind the terrible apparatus of the Inquisition, which seems to have helped in the creation of another monster – witchcraft. There is scarcely a villlage or town in Europe which does not have its own story of witchcraft to tell.

Another story of persecution is that of the Knights Templar, who fell victim to the cupidity of the French monarchy and the papacy mainly because the order itself was so wealthy. Their riches were derived from their vast landholdings in Europe, from their banking enterprises, and from the large fees they collected as guardians of the pilgrims making the dangerous journey from Europe to the Holy Land. It was this wealth which attracted king and pope, yet the true wealth of the Templars was almost invisible, in that it was the wealth which may be seen (by those with eyes to see) on the façades of cathedrals, churches and other buildings which were funded by the riches of the Knights Templar.

From the Knights Templar it is a short step to the masons who, in their operative phase, participated in the building of those arcane structures which we now cathedrals. The story of this phase of European esotericism is complicated because so many of the early masons were also Rosicrucians and alchemists. Some of the Rosicrucian and alchemical images, such as those produced by George Welling, are amongst the most fascinating of arcane symbols.

Those who have neither the means nor the inclination to travel the length of Europe in search of the miraculous may welcome a short list of places of especial interest. Those interested in stone circles might be tempted to visit Stonehenge, though they will find that nowadays its ancient aura of mystery has been lost. A more authentic feeling of the atmosphere of ancient stone circles may be found at Callanish, on the island of Lewis, while some understanding of the vastness of these ancient megaliths may be had among the alignments at Carnac, in France. Those intent on studying the ancient art of the hermetic use of sunlight effects in the service of occult architecture might like to visit the church of San Miniato, in Florence. Those interested in the Cathars could do no better than make the steep climb to the castle of Montségur, or the less arduous trek to the beautiful castle at Lastours, in France. Those intrigued by the history of witchcraft could spend a profitable day wandering among the medieval buildings of Bamberg in Germany, while those interested in the Rosicrucian movement might like to visit the mystical castle at Heidelberg. Cressac, in France, is the ideal place for someone who would wish to capture the essence of the Knights Templar, though the Templar Museum at La Rochelle gives more direct information about the order. Those intrigued by astrology might choose to make a pilgrimage to the mountain-top eyrie of Sacra di San Michele, in Italy, where the earliest zodiacal sculptures in Europe may be found. Anyone wanting to know more about zodiacal clocks could do no better than visit the calendrical system beneath the Palazzo della Ragione in the Citta Alta, at Bergamo. Those fascinated by secret alphabets and symbols are advised to visit the rune stones of Gotland. Those who have no fear of seeking out images of demons would be well advised to spend a morning at Notre-Dame, in Paris, distinguishing the demonic images from there merely alchemical. Those who do not want to seek out any particular occult theme, but would rather experience a mystery centre which has a distinctive and undeniably spiritual atmosphere, from its position on leys, orientation lines and other telluric currents, are advised to spend a full day walking on the sand dunes around Mont St-Michel, in northern France: a visit to the walled city itself is perhaps less rewarding, for it has been washed clean of spiritual force by tourism.

No matter where you are in Europe, you cannot be very far from one or another of the great mystery centres, which were designed to inform and enlarge the soul of man. Such buildings and symbols speak an unfamiliar language, with the result that, more often than not, mankind walks by without hearing, seeing or sensing their inner meaning. A true appreciation of the meaning of a genuine mystery centre can be had only when one has developed the inner and outer eyes with which to see. Perhaps this book will help nurture this special kind of vision so necessary to the real appreciation of the spiritual wonders of our world.

1 Heretics and Knights

The distinctive tower of the cathedral at Albi, the city from which the Albigensian movement took its name.

Overleaf: the great medieval walled town of Carcassonne, one of the most important of the centres of Albigensianism.

IN the south of France there are many walled towns and cities which still evoke the atmosphere of earlier days, when they were linked with one of the most terrible, yet fascinating periods in the history of the Christian religion. It was in this area that the heretical sect known as the Cathars, or Albigensians, were most powerful, during the eleventh and twelfth centuries.

The Albigensians took their name from the city of Albi which was their most important stronghold, but these heretics had many names – usually related to their place of origin. For example, the Agennenses were from Agen, not far from Albi, while the Concorricci were from the town of Concorrazzo, near Monza, the Albanenses were from Alba, and the Bagnolenses from Bagnolo, near Brescia, three towns in Italy.

Occultists and esoteric groups have a particular fondness for the Albigensians, since the roots of their heresy are found in the same dualism which exists behind most occult systems. The origins of the Albigensian heresy lay in the Manichaean dualism and Gnosticism of the third century, which had occult and magical overtones and stemmed from the idea that all worldly phenomena are a result of the opposition between Light and Darkness, between Good and Evil. In particular, the Manichaeans held that God and the Devil had equal power – a notion utterly abhorrent to the teachings of the Christian Church, which proclaimed God as the supreme being, with even the Devil under his control. For all its pronounced view of this cosmic state of affairs, the Church had always been ambivalent about the relationship between Good and Evil, however: if God had been in complete control of Eden, then there would have been no Fall, and therefore no need for the Redeemer, Christ. The issue at stake was essentially the view one took of human freedom – did the fact that Eve succumbed to the temptations of the Serpent lead not only to the Fall but also to the beginnings of human freedom? Indeed, was the role of the Devil, represented here by the serpent, an agent of free will? The issues were frequently discussed within the Church, yet the anomalies to which they pointed were never resolved. The heretical stream, which rested on a dualism earlier than Christianity, resolved the problem to some extent by visualising God and the Devil in opposition, with the Devil as the actual creator of the material world. This view, so contrary to established Church doctrine, was inevitably to lead to conflict between the two groups.

THE BACKGROUND TO HERESY

Although historians are faced with the problem that almost everything which is known about the Cathars is derived from the writings of their enemies (the medieval Church), they have still been able to determine the most important of their heretical beliefs. These heresies (beliefs contrary to those taught by the Catholic Church) included denial of, the Virgin Birth, the efficacy of baptism, the power of saintly relics, the real presence of the Eucharist, the lawfulness of marriage, the remission of original sin by the act of baptism, the power of the symbol of the Holy Cross, and of the notion that prayers for the dead are effectual.

Many of the beliefs and attitudes of the Albigensians during the twelfth and thirteenth centuries clearly arose from a reaction to the corruption of the contemporary Catholic Church, and a suspicion of the worldly power it openly espoused. The Albigensians' antagonism seems not to have been directed against Christianity as such, but against the maladministration of the Church, at what they regarded as certain misinterpretations of the Gospels, and at the immorality and laxity of the priesthood. They did not actually deny Christ, as their accusers claim, but regarded him as God made Man. It is clear that they believed that only the development of moral purity would enable Mankind to escape the clutches of the Devil; they were, indeed, sometimes called the Cathars, from a Greek word meaning pure ones. In contrast, many of the Catholic clergy were far from moral: 'nothing was more common than for monks even, and regular canons, to cast aside their attire, take to gambling and hunting, consort with concubines, and turn jugglers or doctors'. These are not the words of a heretic criticising the Church but of Pope Innocent III, who saw in such behaviour the reasons for the rapid spread of heresy throughout Europe. An ironic comparison between heretic and churchman may be observed in a story which tells how, in 1157, the Bishop of Reims discovered a group of Albigensian heretics when a local girl refused to submit to the sexual demands of one of his young clerics. Such a refusal was regarded as being extremely unconventional by the Church, and when the girl was asked to explain herself, she called in her friends to support her belief in the importance of virginity. The astounded ecclesiastical authorities promptly arrested them all as heretics.

Eventually, the spread of the Albigensian heresy was such that, numerically speaking, it threatened the actual supremacy of the Church itself, and this led to open enmity – and even to armed conflict – between the heretics and the Catholics. This was more or less inevitable, not just because of the doctrinal differences between the two groups, but also because of the growing hostility of the heretics towards the church they believed to be corrupt. In a discourse between Catholics and heretics, held in Montréal near Carcassonne, Oton, an Albigensian priest, proclaimed in public that the Church of Rome was nothing more than the feared Babylon of the Apocalypse, images of which were widespread in medieval times. In the early years of the heresy, the church contented itself with excommunicating the heretics, but eventually witch-hunts were organised which resulted in the torture and burning of isolated groups. Thus in 1049, all those who had gathered for safety in the Montwiner fortress in Chalons were excommunicated, but a few years later most of the inhabitants of Béziers were massacred. In 1125 a peasant from Bucy near Soissons gathered a considerable following: he taught that Christ was but a phantasm (a notion which actually harks back to the earliest-known heresy, now called Docetism), that the altar was 'the mouth of hell', and the Christian mysteries without value. This peasant, described by the Count of Soissons to be the wisest man he knew, was imprisoned for life. In 1167, an heretical group was rounded up and tried at Vezelay; after the ordeal of water, one was set free, but seven were burnt. At Orvieto, in 1200, a papal legate sent to restrain the heresy was actually put to death by the townspeople, while the resistance in Viterbo was so strong that it took the presence of the Pope himself, who organised the destruction of the heretics' property, to restore order.

In 1207, after a couple of years fruitlessly spent in attempting to convert the heretics by preaching, Innocent III proclaimed a Crusade against their strongholds in the south of France. This European crusade resulted in the worst rapine and massacre witnessed on European soil since the collapse of the Roman Empire. When the city of Béziers was taken by the Catholic forces, the victors were ordered to kill everyone – heretics and Catholics alike – on the grounds that 'the Lord would recognize his own'. Narbonne was not taken by these 'crusaders', but was saved from destruction only when its inhabitants (seemingly with reluctance) executed large numbers of the heretics who had until then lived peacefully within its walls. The holocaust was not restricted to France, however: in 1163 there was a wholesale burning of Cathars in Cologne.

The memorial to the Cathars at Minerve.

The courage of the heretics was often extraordinary: in the fortress of Minerve, 140 of their number, recognising that their cause was lost, threw themselves on a pyre rather than fall into the hands of the Catholic soldiers: a rock, pierced with a beautiful carving of a dove, now marks the spot where these men and women died. In Lavaur where the military carried out terrible atrocities, the Governor and 80 of his knights who had surrendered were executed in a single day. At Marmande over 5,000 men, women and children were barbarically killed on the orders of the Bishop of Saints, even though there was little evidence that they were all heretics. At the end of the first phase of these military operations, the Pope could boast that 500 towns and castles had been brought back into the fold of the Catholic Church.

Throughout the early struggles and the whole period of the European Crusade the most important leader of the heretics was Raymond VI, Count of Toulouse, who was excommunicated on three separate occasions. When Raymond died in 1222 the Church forbade his burial in consecrated ground, and for nearly 150 years his remains lay exposed to sight within the precincts of the Hospital of the Knights of St John, outside Toulouse; it was perhaps the longest intentionally delayed burial in history.

In recent years, the Cathars have been acclaimed as heroes, and even taken as revolutionary democrats, with the result that several places in southern France have laid claim to nourishing the heresy. While some of these claims are dubious, there are several fortified hill-towns and villages – mainly in a ruined state – which have strong historical links with these religious rebels. Many of these places are still difficult of access, and it is not easy to understand how they were ever taken by a besieging army. Among the most impressive, and well worth the effort of the hard climb, are the four towers at Lastours, the extraordinary balancing-act of Montségur, and the lovely castle of Peyrepertuse. More accessible, and consequently more subject to the ravages of tourism, is the medieval walled city of Carcassone, a renowned centre of heresy, which was besieged several times.

At the hill-village of Minerve, with the ruined remains of its old castle, some effort has been made to meet the modern demand for information. A small museum, mainly of figurines and landscapes, has been mounted in the rue des Martyrs, not far from the Cathar dove-stone in front of the twelfth-century church mentioned above.

A view of the most inaccessible of all the Catharian strongholds – the mountain-top castle of Montségur. Even today, when a pathway has been cut up to the ruins, the climb is far from being an easy one.

The ruins of the old Catharian centre at Lastours consists essentially of four towers, each of which may be visited, after a considerable climb up and around the peak on which the complex of Lastours stands. Records indicate that after the Cathars had been wiped out by the Papal forces, the fortifications were taken over as strongholds by the Knights Templar.

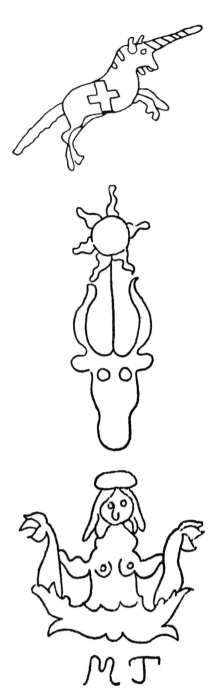

According to the esoteric historian Harold Bayley, the watermarks used by the medieval papermarks of southern France consisted of esoteric devices which incorporated meanings clear to the heretics but hidden from their persecutors. The selection above, from Bayley's book, gives a few examples of this secret code, including the unicorn, a bull's head, and a siren.

THE TAROT

Some occultists have attempted to trace the designs of that curious divinatory pack of cards, the Tarot, to the French and Italian heretical schools, perhaps because the original designs of the cards appear to have had symbols of a dualist nature. The task of tracing occult origins in the Tarot designs is a difficult one, mainly because there is a great deal of evidence to suggest that the cards were first used just for playing games; it was not until the sixteenth century that they were employed for reading the future. Even then, contemporary references suggest they were used in the same way as ordinary playing cards, which were certainly not designed on occult principles.

The possible connection between the Tarot and general cartomancy does not appear to have been explored however, though this link is suggested by the fact that the gypsies were reputed to have brought the Tarot and its divinatory methods from the East. In fact, the heretical movement of the Athinganists is first recorded in the eighth century in Europe, and as far as may be determined they had preserved many of the Gnostic traditions, although still observing the Jewish Sabbath. They are reputed to have worshipped the demons, Sorou, Sochen and Arche, all names which appear to be corruptions of Graeco-Gnostic terms. They were famous as practitioners of magic and astrology, and it is probably for this reason that their name was given to the Gypsies — the French for gypsy, *tsigane* being merely the 'Athinganus'. However, as Steven Runciman points out in his book *The Medieval Manichee,* the true gypsies (the Romanies) did not appear in Anatolia (as emigrants from India) until the ninth century. Astrology and other popular forms of divination were widely practised at this time, even though considered inadvisable in the East by the Koran, and frowned upon by the Catholic Church. It is possible that the origins of the Tarot card designs, which first appeared in Europe in the fourteenth century, may lie in the activities of these or similar heretical movements.

Another interesting, and perhaps unexpected, source of Tarot imagery may be found in certain papermarks. Occult historians recognise that the medieval paper-makers of southern France were much given to heresy, and the symbols they introduced as watermarks are so similar to certain symbols on Gnostic amulets that the resemblance cannot be merely accidental. The great occult historian Harold Bayley, in his work *The Lost Language of Symbolism,* refers to designs such as those found in the fabric of paper as 'thought-fossils or thought-crystals, in which lie enshrined the aspirations and traditions of the numerous mystic and puritanic sects by which Europe was overrun in the Middle Ages'. He links the puritanic sects specifically with the Albigensians of France and the Patarini sects of Italy, and the claims that the use of such emblems as watermarks was one way in which the persecuted heretics were able to preserve their secret symbolism in the face of opposition from the Church. As at least two examples on this page indicate, there is a connection between some of the early watermarks and the symbols later adopted by the Freemasons. Many occultists maintain that the lore of the Templars, Albigensians and the Rosicrucians was later adopted and transformed by the Freemasons, which is why one may so easily trace a connection between the symbols used by the earliest of Europe's papermakers and those still used by Masons.

Later historians have recognised that there is also a link between these watermark symbols and some of the heraldic devices used on the Tarot cards. A close study of the early Tarot packs made by the American historian, Stuart Kaplan, has revealed that in the early days certain heraldic devices appeared on the cards, some of which are remarkably similar to the watermarks used by the Albigensian papermakers in earlier centuries. Among these devices is the Visconti Viper which, besides appearing on the cards, is found on several church façades in northern Italy linked with the Visconti family of Milan. In one version the Visconti Viper is shown as a curved basilisk which is swallowing a human being, its breast bearing what is probably a six-pointed star. In some examples the viper (which is, of course, a basilisk) is alone, without its grisly meal. In other examples of the Visconti heraldic devices the viper is represented as a winged dragon, but still swallowing its human victim. To the occultist this symbol is of great interest because the image of a snake devouring a man is a standard symbol of initiation. Its meaning is that a true initiate is one who is as familiar with the outer world as with

Six late-medieval Tarot cards (Major Arcana) preserved in the Museum at Piacenza. The top row, from left to right, shows The Star, The (unnamed) Death card, and The Angel; the bottom row shows The Justice, The Moon, and The Chariot.

the hidden inner one, so that a picture of someone who is both 'within' and 'without' – especially an image of someone being swallowed by the serpent of wisdom – is designed to point to a successful initiation. Many occultists recognise that a number of the powerful families who dominated the political and spiritual life in Italy prior to and during the Renaissance were themselves directly linked with initiation centres, so it is perhaps not surprising to see such an heraldic device on the arms of the most powerful of all Milanese families.

The first written reference to the Tarot cards (*Carte de Triumphi* in the early Italian terminology) was in 1450, in a transcript of a letter written by Francesco Sforza, Duke of Milan. It is interesting that in a series of frescoes in the Casa Borromeo in Milan, one picture shows a group of aristocrats playing a game with these cards – they are clearly not being used for prediction at all. Almost certainly, the Tarot cards referred to by Francesco Sforza were probably of the kind now classified by historians as the Visconti and Visconti-Sforza series, a fine collection of which are in the Accademia Carrara in Bergamo. Other important collections, also in Italy, are in the Museo delle Arti e delle Tradizioni Popolari in Rome, the Castello Sforzesco in Milan, and (on public display) in the City Museum, Piacenza.

As Stuart Kaplan points out, literary evidence indicates that the Tarot was not used for fortune telling until as late as 1527. However many popular historians of this curious art have been prepared to ignore this fact and rewrite history to fit their own wild imaginings. The most influential of these was the Frenchman, Antoine Court de Gébelin, writing in the 18th century, who suggested an origin of impossible antiquity and, in spite of all the iconography, an Egyptian origin. This wild guesswork somehow came at the right time, and many occultists (presumably unlearned in history) have adopted these notions. Of course, there were many different Tarot designs, but the most popular and frequently encountered design is the one known nowadays as the 'Marseilles pack'. It was first printed in large numbers in that city, and has been adopted by many clairvoyants for its especially meaningful graphic symbols which act as what Jung has called autoscopes.

The Popesse Card of the Tarot pack, sometimes called The Lady Pope or The Pope Joan.

A detail from the life of the mythical Pope Joan, who is shown hanging from a gallows, with her child in her arms. From a sixteenth-century woodprint.

The Café Procope, said to be the oldest of all Parisian cafés, is often pointed out as the place where Court de Gébelin would meet his occultist brethren and discuss esoteric matters. This café was also frequented by at least one other occultist who was to have a profound influence on esoteric thought and magic in the nineteenth century; this was Alponse Louis Constant, better known by his *nom de plume* of Éliphas Lévi. It was Lévi who traced Court de Gebelin's picture book of Thoth to the Hebrews, by constructing a series of quite imaginative cabbalistic associations which have become part and parcel of Tarot symbolism.

One of the iconographic mysteries of the Tarot pack is the curious Lady Pope card. Although some Catholics may take exception to the notion of a female pontiff, the truth is that in medieval art the image of a woman wearing a triple tiara is sometimes used to represent the Church herself. It is unlikely that such a picture was intended as an affront, or even that it is especially occult in some mysterious way. Even so, at least one modern historian of the Tarot has pointed to a similarity between the card and an image of the Egyptian goddess Isis in the Borgia Apartment at the Vatican in Rome. It shows the Egyptian goddess seated on a throne, with an open book on her lap, flanked by two pillars, in much the same relationship of symbols as on the Marseilles design.

In the ninth century, Anastasius, librarian of the Vatican, left a reference to a supposed Pope Joan which gained some notoriety, but which has since been revealed as a throwback to a myth derived from an old folk-tale. This female Pope was said to have been born in Metz and, under the name of Joannes Anglicus, was educated in Cologne, and raised to the Papacy in the mid-ninth century, reigning for two years, five months and four days. The image of the Lady Pope holding a child in her arms and hanging from a gallows over the mouth of hell, with demons in attendance, is from a poem by Jacobus Egmonden about the Popes. He includes Pope Joan (actually 'Johannes') and recounts the legend of her giving birth to a child near St Clement's Church, which is close to the Colosseum in Rome.

Hieronymus Bosch – a detail from
The Temptation of St Anthony in
the National Museum, Lisbon. The
strange imagery in Bosch's pictures
has been explained in many ways,
but perhaps the most persuasive
explanation is that he worked for
an esoteric school regarded as
heretical by the Catholic church.

HIERONYMUS BOSCH

The extraordinary paintings of Hieronymus Bosch, so obviously filled with arcane
symbolism, are often taken by occultists as examples of occult or heretical art. Even
reputable art historians, who wisely tend to fight shy of the history of occultism, have
attempted to show a connection between Bosch and certain heretical schools; for
example Wilhelm Fraenger in his book *The Millenium of Hieronymus Bosch*, has
convincingly argued that *The Garden of Earthly Delights*, Bosch's masterpiece in the
Prado, Madrid, was designed for an heretical group called the Adamites.

It is in the Prado that the occult world of Bosch is best studied, for here his
diabolical landscapes, *The Haywain* and *The Garden of Earthly Delights* are on
permanent display. There is no doubt that Bosch's work, while reflecting contemporary
views on alchemy, witchcraft and astrology, was linked with an heretical school, even if

it was not the one suggested by Fraenger. The Brethren of the Free Spirits, as the Adamites were sometimes called, were supposed to have worshipped naked and may have indulged in rites involving more liberal sexual practices than the medieval world held proper. Bosch worked in 's-Hertogenbosch in Holland, not far from the Belgian border, and it is quite possible that the complex series of demonic figures and gargoyles on the cathedral of St John there, influenced his view of the spiritual and demonic realm at a formative stage.

Less directly arcane than the works of Bosch, however, are the few known paintings by his contemporary, Herri Met de Bles. A beautiful sixteenth-century roundel by this master in the Mauritshaus in The Hague, was almost certainly painted for the Adamites or a related heretical group; it certainly contains esoteric symbols which would not be recognised by the established Church. A detail from this panel, showing Eve taking the fruit from the Serpent, contains interesting iconographic references which mark the picture as being heretical. A goat, always associated with lasciviousness, and which has an established connection with the sabbat, stares up at the naked couple. Directly over the image of the Moon (which is in opposition to the Sun, on the far edge of the roundel), a dog barks at the hog, indicating that discord between the animals, which is traditionally associated with the Fall of Man, has already been introduced into the world. It is interesting to compare this image of two animals snarling at each other with The Moon card from the Marseilles Tarot, which depicts two dogs preparing to fight beneath a full Moon. The symbolism of this mysterious card has never been fully explained, yet it is clearly linked with such iconographic details as we find in the Met de Bles roundel.

THE HOLY GRAIL AND THE ROUND TABLE

The Albigensian stronghold of Montségur — together with several other historical Albigensian sites — has become associated with the Grail legends and the tales of Arthur and the Knights of the Round Table in recent years. Such is the confusion surrounding these three different elements — Albigensians, Holy Grail and Arthurian romance — that it is useful to disentangle the threads.

The existence of the Albigensians (and Cathars) is of course an historical fact. Linking the Holy Grail to their known beliefs — as several modern occultists have done — is a little uncomfortable since the Grail as a Christian symbol is clearly linked with the Blood and Wine of Holy Communion: a sacrament emphatically rejected by the Albigensians. However the specifically Christian associations of the Grail cannot be traced earlier than the romance *Joseph of Arimathea*, written by Robert de Borron in the twelfth century. In mythology, a multiplicity of evolved forms usually implies great antiquity. The many forms which the Grail takes in different tales and myths — chalice, plate, head, stone, etc. — clearly identifiy it as a relic of pre-Christian religion.

While Robert de Borron was busy Christianizing the Grail, other twelfth-century writers (notably Wace in France and Layamon in England) were reworking the Arthurian legends to embrace not only Christianity but also the Grail, which did not feature in many of the (numerous and bewilderingly diverse) stories of Arthur. Arthur, like the Grail, is certainly much older than Christianity. The theme of the fisher king whose life and death are inextricably bound up with his land and people is strikingly similar to the ancient cults associated with deities such as Adonis and Attis.

By showing that the Grail and Arthur pre-date Christianity we have not proved that they had no connection with a specifically Christian heresy. What we have done is to open up to speculation a series of much more exciting possibilities.

Jesus was himself a Dying God, as were Attis and Adonis. He was nailed to a tree, like Odin. The ideas and rituals of Christianity (as adapted by Saint Paul) spread quickly throughout the Roman Empire. Perhaps this comparatively rapid acceptance of the new god among pagan peoples was because Christianity had many similarities with their existing patterns of worship. Perhaps the Albigensians were not heretics swerving from the path of Christian orthodoxy, but conservatives who had been worshipping their god in the same manner for many centuries before the birth of Christ, and who rejected some of the new doctrines which accompanied worship of the Nazarene.

A striking detail from one of the fountains in the main square of Beaufort-en-Vallée, a place intimately connected with the esoteric legends of Arthur and the Holy Grail – the castle on the hill behind the town is said to have been the birthplace of Lancelot.

Nor does any of this speculation undermine the essential doctrine of Christianity. On the contrary, it draws strength from its assurance with myths and rituals as old as Mankind. Little remains of the buildings featured in the original Grail legends in France or Germany (an exception being the ruined castle above the Goetheanum, near Dornach), though several castles are said to be linked with the legendary knights. The hilltop castle at Beaufort-en-Vallée is still revered as the place where Sir Lancelot du Lac was born, and many of the details of sculpture and ironwork in the town below would suggest a lively interest in things occult, from the gargoyles of the church to the metal snakes on the town's fountain, and from the statue of the grape goddess in the small square behind the church, to the stained glass windows dedicated to Joan of Arc inside the church.

THE ESTABLISHMENT OF THE INQUISITION

From the point of view of the history of occultism – especially in connection with the study of witchcraft, a diabolical art all too often linked with the Albigensians by their detractors – the consequence of the European Crusade was interesting in its ominous repercussions. Until the early part of the thirteenth century, the legal system in Europe was based on that of ancient Rome. This required that for a person to be tried in a court of law there had to be someone to come forward to make an accusation. Since most people were not terribly interested in heresy, nor sufficiently educated to recognise its existence, and since heretics themselves tended to be fairly secretive (certainly clinging together in adversity) – accusations were rarely made against them, save by interested members of the Church. Therefore, from the point of view of the Catholic Church at least, the old Roman system was proving more and more inefficient in curbing heresy. To get around this difficulty, the Pope decided to establish a new legal body, formed to establish a system of inquiry which would supplement the method of 'accusation'. The new body was charged with gathering information – openly and in secret – and with establishing a technical procedure for formulating a distinct legal charge; it was a development which would render the old system more 'workable', in that it could hardly fail to obtain convictions. Since this official body would be empowered to torture suspects in the course of its inquiries, its power was formidable, and as Innocent III suspected, by its agency it was possible for the Church to establish a new and quite frightening form of justice in Europe. The body charged with establishing this form of inquiry, and empowered to root out all forms of heresy, was called the Inquisition.

The establishment of this legal ecclesiastical body, which was to have extraordinary consequences for the development of European history, did not take place overnight, yet by 1229 the brainchild of Pope Innocent III had the necessary powers to enable its prosecution of all forms of heresy – real or imagined – throughout any part of Europe under the control of the Catholic Church. It was from this time that the witch-hunts began in Europe (see page 61), for the evidence suggests that the mechanism established to eradicate the Albigensian heretics, having done its work most thoroughly, had to turn its attention to other forms of 'heresy' in order to maintain its role. It was not difficult for the Inquisition, learned in countering the ways of an heretical body which denied so many of the tenets of the Catholic Church, to see similar patterns in witchcraft; both seemed designed to destroy God's Church, and both questioned His role as the true Creator.

THE KNIGHTS TEMPLAR

Within the framework of the Church, the largest body to fall victim to the Inquisition was the Templars. The Knights Templar (or, to give them their full name, The Military Order of the Knights of the Temple of Solomon), were a military religious order, founded in 1119 shortly after the opening of the great religious routes to the Holy Land. Their role was to guard these routes from brigands and Muslim raiders, and their religious Rule was determined by 72 articles, the number 72 being of special astrological significance since the sun retrogrades against the zodiac exactly one degree in 72 years. Through their activities in the Middle East they built up vast wealth based on the acquisition of land and on banking. It was undoubtedly this wealth which led to their undoing, for it attracted the greed of both Church and State.

When the Christians were driven out of Palestine by the Mameluks of Egypt, the Templars were deprived of their main purpose. However, even before that time their usefulness was in question: the French King, and even the Pope, had shown a less than moral interest in their considerable riches. In 1307 the French members of the order were arrested in the name of the Inquisition, at the behest of King Philip IV who immediately took over the management (and proceeds) of their properties and wealth. The Knights were arraigned on a number of charges, most of which concerned heresies including the standard Denial of Christ (which had been more legitimately levelled against the Albigensians), idol worship and homosexuality. The Grand Master of the Order, Jacques de Molay, was among those arrested and subjected to terrible torture. It seems that he, and those tortured with him, confessed to all the crimes of which they

One of the waxen seals of the Knights Templar which portrays two knights astride a single horse, perhaps a symbol of the vow of poverty and humility which was originally enforced upon the order. From the Templar Museum, La Rochelle.

were accused, thereby condemning themselves as heretics.

The arrests of the Templars had not been formally authorised by the Pope, but faced with the situation, Clement V decided to side with the French monarchy and agree to the charges – though the sequestration of their extensive properties was (naturally) claimed in the name of the Pope, rather than the King. As a result of his intervention, the papal legates visited the Knights in prison, at which point the unfortunate men all withdrew their confessions, believing that (as the nominal head of their order) the Pope would release them. They were not released, however, and afterwards it became apparent to members of the Order that they had been betrayed by King and Pope alike. By 1310 about 600 Templars had retracted their 'confessions' and decided to defend their Order in the courts. On 12 May 1310, without further trials, 54 were burned in Paris, and some of their leaders disappeared in mysterious circumstances.

In 1312 the Order was suppressed by the Pope, and Jacques de Molay, who still insisted on protesting his own and the Order's innocence, was burned at the stake on the Ile des Javiaux, in the Seine. As Malcolm Barber reports in *The Trial of the Templars*, they died heroically, and their deaths quickly resulted in a series of legends. Pope Clement V died on 20 April, while Philip IV followed on 29 November of the same year. It was said that Jacques de Molay had called them both to appear with him before the tribunal of God. Whatever happened in the Heavens, on earth the ashes of the Grand Master were collected by friars and other religious persons, and taken away to holy places as sacred relics.

TEMPLAR LEGENDS

The esoteric tradition has embellished such legends and made much of the Knights Templar. The Temple of Solomon is regarded as an occult structure, designed in such a way as to reflect the cosmos and with a tradition still active in Masonic circles; the order of the Knights Templar itself has been described as a ruling body, founded on secret principles and dedicated to the teaching of those occult principles often described as 'esoteric Christianity'.

Such claims, made by esotericists like Fulcanelli, are not difficult to substantiate, for example by studying the Templar imagery in many French churches and cathedrals.

A detail from the façade of Chartres
cathedral, showing two different
strains of symbolism (see page 25).

Undoubtedly, the most impressive centre of this sort is at Chartres, in northern France, where the imagery of the Templars has been closely integrated with that of the zodiac. On the northernmost door of the cathedral's West front the typanum bears images of ten signs of the zodiac. The missing two signs – Gemini and Pisces – have been moved to the southern door of the West front. This dispersal of symbols was quite intentional, as the architect was intent on proclaiming the special importance of both Gemini and Pisces to Chartres. The image for Gemini is unconventional in that it depicts two men (the Twins) using a single shield. This is a direct reference to the seal of the Knights Templar which portrays two knights sharing a single horse, (a reference perhaps to their sense of brotherhood and communal purpose).

The pointed bottom of this shield is directed to another symbol, which is almost hidden behind the moulding: this is a single fish, intended to represent Pisces. The fish itself is portrayed singly, rather than in the more common dual form, because it is intended to represent Christ as well as the zodiacal sign. From very early times, the fish has been used as a symbol for Christ, perhaps on the grounds that Christ inaugurated the Age of Pisces (under which influence Mankind is still placed). The interesting thing about this single fish is that it cannot easily be seen because of the moulding – in order to view it it is necessary to move back into the square (across the road in front of the cathedral). However, even at this distance the fish is almost too small to be seen clearly. This fish is 'hidden', not merely in the sense that it has been hidden from the rest of the zodiac on the other portal, but also in that it is hard to see. Taken together, the Gemini-Pisces symbols at Chartres may be seen as a direct reference to the Knights Templars, guardians of the *hidden* Christian knowledge.

Since the trials of the Templars, legends have circulated to the effect that the Knights worshipped a strange head, called by some a 'maumet'. A few of the Knights, while under torture, confessed to using it in their rituals, including Étienne de Troyes, who also repeated the old *canard* that, at his initiation ceremony, he had been compelled to appear naked and kiss another knight 'on the lower spine'. The strange head, to which he claimed to have witnessed a ritual of homage, seemed to be 'flesh from the crown to the nape of the neck with the hairs of a dog without any gold or silver covering, indeed a face of flesh . . . bluish in colour and stained, with a beard having a mixture of white and black hairs similar to the beards of some Templars'. Some claim the word 'maumet' derives from the name of the Holy Prophet Mohammed, the founder of Islam, who was feared by the Western world during the times of the Crusades as 'a Muslim God'. This maumet may indeed have been a human relic, perhaps even the preserved head of one of the founders of the Order, Hugh de Payens, which is known to have been kept by the Templars in a precious reliquary. A sculpture of a winged demon, with short horns and well-developed breasts, in the church of St Merri (not far from the more famous tower of St Jacques in Paris), is often said to be a representation of this maumet: however, St Merri (the name being a corruption of Mederic, a seventh-century monk) was not built until the early sixteenth century, and therefore cannot have had anything to do with the original Templars. Even so, one cannot help wondering if it was this sculpture which influenced the magician Éliphas Lévi (see page 18) when he drew his own famous Baphomet. A more convincing 'Baphomet' may be traced in the horned head on the Templar *commanderie* of St-Bris-le-Vineux.

The notion of the Baphomet head entered into popular occultism in a way which separated its imagery from the original religious intentions of the Knights Templar. An extreme example of this division may be seen in the monstrous image called 'Baphomet' illustrated above, in which we may trace a human head, the head of a ram, that of a cock, bird feet and wings, and what may be priapus – all symbols more obviously linked with Gnostic occult speculation than anything to do with the Templars. The modern magician Aleister Crowley adopted this seal in 1912 when Theodor Reuss made him head of an esoteric order (then in decline) called Ordo Templi Orientalis. The worship of the priapus (especially his own) was an important element in Crowley's life, and it is said that the members of the Ordo worshipped a statuette of an erect penis upon their altars. The order was suppressed by the Nazis in 1937, by which time it was more or less defunct. However, at no time did it appear to represent any of the high spiritual ideals of the original Templars.

Seal of the Grand Master of the secret order Ordo Templi Orientalis, adopted by Aleister Crowley when he was allegedly made Master of the Order in 1912. Although called Baphomet, the figure has nothing to do with genuine Templar imagery.

THE 'HIDDEN' WEALTH OF THE TEMPLARS

It is not surprising that an order like the Templars which, during its existence, was so invested with esoteric legends, has been laden with even more mythology in later times. In this respect, the legendary wealth of the Order has given rise to much imaginative speculation as to its present location, but the truth is that most of the silver and gold, and certainly all the lands, were appropriated by the Papacy and secular authorities long before the unsuspecting Knights could hide any of it. The reason why the Knights (who were, after all, military monks) were arrested with such ease was mainly because they had no warning whatsoever: the Master, Jacques de Molay, had actually been officiating at a royal reception immediately before his arrest, for it was part of the King's plan to give the Order no time to hide the possessions after which he lusted.

The temples of the Order have left their names, and sometimes their original buildings remain, in several parts of Europe. In England the most famous is the Temple Church, to the south of Fleet Street in London, in which the cross-legged knightly effigies are said (quite erroneously) to represent Templars, or at least crusaders. One image which may safely be identified as truly representing a Templar is in the fresco of the ancient Templar church at Cressac, which portrays the wars between the knights and the Saracens.

Even in those areas where the Templars were strong, few remains are found. However, at La Rochelle, near the old port, in the tower of La Grosse Horloge, is a museum nominally given over to the history of the Templars, though in fact concentrating mainly on local Templar sites. Among the exhibits are some interesting documents, a few with ancient seals, including one based on the double-rider theme, and a selection of photographs of churches and symbols which survive today. Anyone interested in making a study of the Templars in the south-west of France is well advised to visit this museum first.

One of the effigies in the Temple Church, off Fleet Street in London. Though frequently associated with the Templars, these are probably memorials to ordinary knights and crusaders. It is said that there is only one effigy which is undoubtedly that of a Knight Templar, which is in Soissons, in France.

A rare image of a Templar – a late thirteenth-century fresco in the small Templar church at Cressac, which portrays the knights fighting with the Saracens.

Below: a view of the dome of La Grosse Horloge from across the harbour at La Rochelle, where the Templar Museum is housed.

A Templar document (seal now
removed) from the display in the
Templar Museum in La Rochelle.
The complex signatures at the
bottom right of the parchment are
typical of Templar script.

Below: the Templar church at
Laon, which is one of the best
preserved in northern France.

Among the Templar establishments listed near Angoulême is the fascinating church at Cressac, with the aforementioned frescoes: unfortunately, these have been restored in relatively modern times, and many of the symbols incorporated into the imagery are not genuine. Some authorities have pointed to the fact that the images of the fighting knights recall the almost contemporary reliefs on the façade of Angoulême cathedral. However, the truth is that these latter knights are not Templars, as is often believed, but illustrate a romantic epic relating to Roland of Roncevaux (Chanson de Roland) at the taking of Saragossa from the Arabs. One set of bas reliefs which do have a direct link with the Knights Templar, though, are found in the Templar Chapel at Villalcázar de Sirga, in Spain, and date more or less from the time when the Order was suppressed. Some people claim the frescoes in the round Templar chapel at Tomar, in Portugal, are of Templar origin, but in fact they postdate the Templar era by almost 300 years.

Among the many impressive Templar churches in France is the one at Laon, which still manages to retain an atmosphere of great sanctity despite the demonic head on a soffit which some claim to represent the maumet. To the south of Bondoubleau is Le Temple, where stands a twelfth-century church once used by the Templars' commanders in this tiny village. More specifically occult is the imagery in the nearby church of St Martin (at Sargé-sur-Braye) for in the chancel there are images of the so-called 'Labours of the Months', which include a most fascinating three-faced Janus, symbolising January. It is usual to explain this imagery in terms of the fact that January marked the 'opening' of the year (the Latin *janua* means doorway). It is said that the god looked with two of his faces into the disappearing past and into the coming future. In St Martin's church, he sups from two bowls, placed to his two pair of lips. There are octagonal Templar chapels at Puy-en-Velay in France, at Tomar in Portugal, and at Eunate on the old pilgrims' route to Santiago, near Pamplona in Spain. All these are worth visits.

Detail of a demon-headed soffit on the south wall of the Templar church at Laon. Although the notion of the Templars worshipping demon heads is almost certainly an untruth promulgated by their persecutors, the fact is that a large number of demonic images are found in connection with Templar imagery.

There are also numerous Templar castles dotting the landscape of France: among the most romantic of which are those at Vaour, which was also associated with the Cathars, and at Coustaussa, which stands like so many giant teeth on the high ground above the village. This place is linked with curious occult legends of modern times, touching on nearby Rennes-le-Château, a village which manages to combine Cathar, Templar, Rosicrucian and occult lore in a bewildering number of stories.

The supposed hidden wealth of the Templars has given rise to many legends, both old and new, and the latest of such myths has lent a spurious and quite undeserved fame to the small hill-village of Rennes-le-Château. This fame is largely the result of romantic

Remains of a Templar building at Vaour which, like Lastours in the same region, was also associated with the Cathars.

stories written about the village and its former occupants, presented as serious history in *The Holy Blood and the Holy Grail* by M. Baigent, R. Leigh and H. Lincoln.

A recent French survey of the mainstream of such romantic inventions (*Rennes-le Château. Le Dossier, Les Impostures, Les Phantasmes, Les Hypotheses* by Gerard de Sede, Paris, 1988) is severe and accurate enough in its criticisms, and, by rights, should lay the ghosts raised by the three modern authors. However, it is evident that the modern penchant for fantasy is unlikely to be deflected by serious historical studies – popular thought has always preferred bizarre hypotheses to cold truth.

If we reject the romances which link Rennes-le-Château with Jesus of Nazareth, and with the untold wealth of the Templars, what is there in the village to excite the interest of esotericists? Perhaps the most interesting thing is the holy water stoup, immediately to the left of the entrance to the church, which is supported by one of the most extraordinary images of the devil in France. This stoup, with its now partially-defaced salamanders, was designed, along with the other restorations inside the church, by l'Abbé Saunière, who is one of the central figures in the modern mythology of Rennes-le-Château. In this restoration, which incorporates many hermetic, Rosi-crucian and masonic symbols, Saunière was aided by the occult sculptor Giscard, whose house in Toulouse, in avenue de la Colonne, is still decorated on the outside with masonic and other hermetic symbols.

Berenger Saunière appeared to have had at his disposal almost endless sums of money which he spent on restoration and building works in the village, and more than enough to make extremely generous gifts to village societies and his friends. Around his wealth, which was certainly not earned in his humble capacity as a priest, there have grown legends of his having discovered the lost wealth of the Templars, the Temple of Solomon itself, or some secret society, and so on. He is even believed to have dug up buried treasure, hidden in the days when Rennes-le-Château was a powerful city. In spite of the many theories, no one has yet been able to determine where his wealth originated, yet the explanations are numerous, often bizarre, and even in modern times treasure hunters and occult theorists are proving something of a bane to the village.

Above left: the silhouette of the Templar castle at Coustaussa, to the north of Rennes-le-Château.

Above right: one of the ruined tower walls of Coustaussa, which stand like so many giant guardians, looking across the valley to the hill-top village of Rennes-le-Château.

Detail of the demon-headed water-stoup placed near the entrance of the church of the Madeleine at Rennes-le-Château on the instructions of l'Abbé Saunière, and designed by the occult sculptor Giscard.

THE HOLY BLOOD

Although ancient tradition insists that after the death of Christ upon the cross the Holy Blood was collected by Joseph of Arimathea – a legend commemorated in the rockface of the German sacred centre at Externsteine – there is no mention of this story in any of the Gospels. However, in an early biography of the holy man Barypsaba, who lived in the fourth century AD, there is a passing reference to a relic of the Holy Blood, a reference which appears to have been confirmed in a now-missing apocryphal Gospel. After the death of Barypsaba, the Holy Blood was supposedly donated to the Byzantine Church at Constantinople. The earliest written record of this relic is no earlier than the eighth century, however. There is no direct literary evidence that this same relic was

Opposite: the curious tower and library-cum-guest-house at Rennes-le-Château, built by l'Abbé Saunière with funds derived from unknown sources.

Images of Thierry of Alsace and his wife Sibyl of Anjou, on the exterior façade of the Basilica of the Holy Blood in Bruges.

the one brought to Bruges by Baldwin X of Flanders, by way of his daughter, the Countess of Flanders, but the connection between the relic and the city of Bruges in medieval times is undoubted.

Indeed, the important society formed in the city of Bruges in the fifteenth century, the Noble Brotherhood of the Holy Blood, almost certainly shared some of the beliefs and opinions of the Templars. In fact, some of the gilded statues on the front of the Basilica of the Holy Blood (Heilig Bloedbaziliek) are sometimes wrongly said to be Templars, perhaps because of the symbols upon their shields. The esoteric aspect of the Brotherhood is related to the preservation and veneration of the phial which, it has been claimed for almost a millenium, contained drops of the Holy Blood, and is still preserved

Detail of stained glass from the Basilica of the Holy Blood, showing the distinctive phial which contains the Holy Blood being buried for safekeeping during a period of unrest in Bruges.

in the basilica at Bruges. The oldest reliable record of this relic dates back to 1150; it is in a list of relics given in a contemporary document, now in the British Library. According to tradition, the relic was brought to Bruges from Constantinople, after the fourth Crusade, by Joan of Constantinople, Countess of Flanders; and records certainly show that by 1256, the relic was already in Bruges. The stained glass inside the two-storey basilica, and the gilded statuary on the façade of the stairway, relate the mystery of the Holy Blood to historical figures. The most lovely of the statues outside are of Thierry of Alsace and his wife, Sibyl of Anjou; he in the livery of a crusader and she holding the mystic Grail containing the Holy Blood. Two different windows depict the discovery of the precious Blood, the oldest stained glass showing the distinctive shape of the bottle itself. The bottle is of rock crystal, and has been dated to the eleventh century: its neck is wound with gold thread, and its stopper sealed with red wax. In turn, this ancient bottle is set in a glass container with gold coronets at each end, ringing a pair of golden angels. The outer container bears the date, in Latin, for 3 May 1388.

The Noble Brotherhood still exists in Bruges; it has 31 members, all of whom must live in the city. They participate in worship, rituals and ceremonies relating to the relic, and also maintain a small but beautiful museum adjoining the church. Of particular interest in the museum is the exquisite gold and silver reliquary of the Holy Blood, designed by Jan Crabbe in 1614, consisting of 35 kilograms of gold and over 100 precious stones. Of special interest to occultists is the cursing horn, which is still sounded on 2 March each year, in memory of Charles the Good who was murdered in 1127. The horn is a reminder of the medieval custom of sounding a musical cursing upon unknown malefactors. In early days there were four horns in Bruges, but the one on display is the only survivor: they were sounded together from the four corners of the square marking the building in which Charles was assassinated. An anonymous painting of of 1528, also on display in the small museum, shows a cursing horn being blown during the Mocking of Christ.

On Ascension Day each year, there is a procession through Bruges in honour of the Holy Blood. The oldest records relating to this procession, contained in a charter of the Torturer's Guild, are dated 1291. The cycle of mystery plays (still enacted at the event) dates back to 1396.

MODERN 'TEMPLAR' ORDERS

Various orders relating to the ideals of the Templars – though all too frequently degenerating into nationalistic sentiment – were established in other European countries, especially in the regions which have since become part of Germany. The memorial to German unity at the Deutsches Eck in Koblenz overlooks a place of great importance to German nationalism – the confluence of the Rhine and the Mosel. The present monument, with its heavy Nordic symbolism, is now topped by the German flag, but originally it was the base for a huge equestrian statue of the Kaiser Wilhelm I: the statue (removed immediately after the end of the Second World War) is still indicated on a bronze plaque set in the ground in front of the monument. There is little doubt that the monument, and the place itself, was a gathering point for the ancient Knights of the Teutonic Order, which was formed in the winter of 1190–1, possibly in the old castle by the Balduinbrucke, now used as the city library. The monument at the Deutsches Eck was erected in 1897, and dedicated to Kaiser Wilhelm I. The symbolic details on its eastern front, oddly reminiscent of Aztec art, show the enormous German eagle dominating six hissing serpents and two cowering human beings.

One of the most recent of the occult groups in Germany to claim some tenuous affiliation with the Templars was the Order of the New Templars, founded towards the end of the nineteenth century by Jörg Lanz von Liebenfels. The 'Order' was perhaps confused in its sense of history, for it merged imaginary Templar rites and symbolism with those believed to belong to the Grail legends. Significantly, however, the Order was anti-semitic and deeply concerned with retaining or developing racial purity among the Nordic peoples. It is clear that Lanz von Liebenfels was one of several pseudo-occultists who introduced certain racialist theories, rooted in the misunderstanding of occult ideas, long before the Nazi Party came to power. Among Lanz von Liebenfels's vast literary output was a ten-volume *Bibliomystikon*, which work

The vast memorial to Kaiser Wilhelm I which stands at the Deutsches Eck, in Koblenz, overlooking the confluence of the Rhine and the Mosel.

purported to be a secret bible for the initiated. In the early part of the present century, it was widely read by the members of Liebenfels's other esoteric creation, Ariosophy.

The earliest sacred site, or 'Temple', purchased by the Order, in 1907, was little more than a ruin overlooking the Danube from Burg Werfenstein in Austria. It is said that Lanz von Liebenfels first raised a flag bearing a swastika in that year, but not a great deal should be made of this for the swastika, fondly believed to have been derived from the sacred Germanic runes, has already been used as a Volkisch symbol for almost a decade. However, the development of the swastika, in relation to such secret fraternities as the Order of New Templars, is dealt with on page 184.

A most interesting fact is that Lanz von Liebenfels (a pseudo-occultist who awarded himself a doctorate in order to impress his public, falsely claimed aristocratic origins, and had once experienced the indignity of being expelled from the Cistercian monastery where he had become a novice) actually met Hitler. This meeting took place in Vienna, in 1909 when the youthful Führer-to-be called on Lanz von Liebenfels to

The old castle on the eastern side of the Balduinbrucke, in Koblenz, where according to tradition the ancient society of the Knights of the Teutonic Order was formed.

collect back numbers of a racialist journal produced by the occultist. In later years, Lanz von Liebenfels claimed that Hitler was, or had been, one of the pupils of the New Templars. However, when the Nazis came to power, and Hitler returned to Austria in a more powerful role, the pseudo-occultist order was driven underground, suffering the same fate as most of the recognised esoteric and hermetic groups in the new Germany. Lanz von Liebenfels himself was forbidden to publish anything further.

The more important members of the Ariosophists were among those other groups – such as the astrologers, faith-healers, radiesthesists, and some of the followers of Steiner – whom the Nazis condemned as occultists. They were arrested by the Gestapo during the purge of astrologers resulting from Aktion Hess, in 1941. None of the Ariosophists

had been particularly famous, or adept in occult matters, save perhaps the palmist Ernst Issberner-Haldane, of Berlin. However, among those arrested and not released was the well-known Swiss astrologer Karl Ernest Krafft. He had correctly predicted that Hitler's life would be endangered on 8 November 1939: the day of an attempted assassination in the Munich Burgerbrau beer cellar. It was Goebbels's interest in this prediction, and in Krafft's undoubted ability, which led to the Swiss astrologer being installed in Berlin to write spurious interpretations of the predictions of Nostradamus, the sage of Paris, to show that, even in the sixteenth century, the great savant recognised that the Master Race was destined to succeed.

Detail of the Aztec-like symbolism on the outer fabric of the Kaiser Wilhelm memorial at the Deutsches Eck, in Koblenz. The vast programme of symbols are intended to reveal mankind, and indeed the cosmic order, under the control of Teutonic supremacy.

2 Demons and Witches

ONE of the most fascinating studies in the history of art and esotericism is that of the iconography of demons and demonology. Almost every European city and town has some trace of demonic lore in one shape or another, either in the form of local legends, details of church architecture (especially gargoyles), or paintings and drawings in art galleries and museums.

Undoubtedly, the most impressive of early demon images are found in Italy, where the arts of fresco painting and mosaic-making were at their height during the Renaissance and the years before – a period which evinced a lively interest in the realm of the nether world. The thirteenth-century mosaic of hell designed by Coppo di Marcovaldo for the octagonal dome of the Baptistry in Florence shows a fearsome subhuman world of demons; a horned Lucifer perches on a serpentine throne, snakes emerging from his ears, his clawed hands clutching at the damned, as he swallows the soul of Judas. Just across the square from the Baptistry is the Duomo, where there is a more restrained vision of hell in the panel which Domenico di Michelino painted in homage to Dante. It shows the lamenting souls being herded into the mouth of hell by giant demons, who appear to be much amused at their human anguish. The eleventh- and twelfth-century mosaics in the cathedral at Torcello are of almost the same high quality, though their imagery is more stark: they depict naked souls burning in the flames of hell, above a frieze of human heads and skulls, with serpents crawling through the empty eye-sockets.

In the Campo Santo of Pisa there is a fresco depicting one of the most frightening of all images of the Devil, his face pitted with forms like eyes. The marvellous series of frescos of the Last Judgement on the walls of the San Brizio chapel in the cathedral of Orvieto, painted by Luca Signorelli at the beginning of the sixteenth century, is a masterpiece of demon-art for the monstrous figures are surrealistically human. In the

Overleaf: the Bishop's *Residenz* in Bamberg, from which the witch-hunts were conducted in the seventeenth century.

The mosaics in the Baptistry, in Florence, contain some of the most powerful of all Christian esoteric symbols. The image of Lucifer devouring Judas Iscariot is one of the most terrifying portrayals of hell in any Christian building.

section showing the preaching of the Antichrist (another popular demonic subject in medieval art), in the first lunette to the left of the chapel there is a portrait of the artist himself.

In France the most memorable images of demons and devils are found in the sculpture of cathedrals and churches, though some of the French frescoes are almost as impressive as those in Italy: for example, the Doom, which portrays horrendous demons carrying off the souls of the damned, in the cathedral at Albi, is of excellent quality. Especially fine examples of façade sculptures are the skeletal demons of Souillac, their emaciated confrères at Autun and the well-fleshed humanoid demons at Bourges, where hell is shown in the form of a huge face, with flames issuing from its mouth, a favourite medieval image.

It is in France that we find one of the most interesting of all memorials to the Devil – the Pont Valentré at Cahors, which was reputably built by His Satanic Majesty himself. The story is an old one, and is told in several places in Europe, but never with such style. According to legend, the building of the Pont Valentré was started in 1308 but, inexplicably, the work dragged on for half a century. In despair at this slow progress, the architect signed a pact with the Devil who, in exchange for his soul, was to bring all the necessary materials to the site immediately. In order to avoid the dreaded final payment, the architect cunningly asked that all the water for the cement-making should be carried in a sieve. Defeated, the Devil showed his frustration by breaking off the topmost stone of the middle fortification, which has ever since been called the Devil's Tower. The final twist to the tale, which makes the bridge at Cahors unique, was added in the nineteenth century. When restorers had finished their own work, they completed the broken tower, firmly attaching to one corner the image of a small demonic figure which is attempting to dislodge the topmost stone.

This detail of the Hell section from the Last Judgement fresco in Orvieto cathedral makes a fascinating contrast with the earlier Florentine mosiac, opposite.

The Pont Valentré at Cahors, one of
the finest medieval bridges still in
existence. The image of the
demonic figure, added by the
nineteenth-century restorers, is on
the northern tower (the nearest in
the picture).

GARGOYLES

The connection between demonic gargoyles and the country of France is preserved
within the word itself, for it comes from the Old French *gargouille*, meaning throat. This
is an appropriate term for these grotesques, for their main function is to spout water
from the roofs of buildings, like so many open mouths. The way in which gargoyles
work can be seen most clearly in France: in a small raised courtyard off rue St Jérôme in
Toulouse, three immense gargoyles from a church wall have been placed on the ground
with their open mouths facing the skies, and their water gutters upright.

Many gargoyles are incorrectly so called, for they do not act as spouts: for
example, the famous beasts, birds and humanoids on the towers of Notre-Dame in Paris
are usually called gargoyles, yet not all these brooding monsters channel water.
Undoubtedly they were intended to perform the role of guardian spirits, and gaze over
the modern city of the Virgin in some puzzlement. A true gargoyle is the one on the
façade of the church of St Hilaire-du-Matray at Loudun, which is well known because it

stared down over the fate of that sad figure, Urbain Grandier, who, in 1643, was wrongly burned for witchcraft (see page 66). Among the most impressive collections of genuine gargoyles are those on the cathedral of St Etienne at Metz, a motley crew that give the impression that they possess a life of their own and will, at any moment, break free from the walls of the cathedral to trouble the world of man. The old port of La Rochelle contains an enormous number of gargoyles and demonic heads – not merely on church walls, but also on the ancient houses in the arcaded streets.

One very surprising demon image in France is the enormous head of Medusa, complete with snake-hair, supporting the arm of no less a person than Leonardo da Vinci. This strange memorial is on the south bank of the Loire valley, at Amboise, where the artist spent the last few years of his life. The manor of Le Clos-Lucé, the house where he lived and died, is also well worth a visit for the exhibition of models constructed from sketches of his inventions, which is mounted in the gardens.

The famous gargoyles on the façade, towers, walls and buttresses of Notre-Dame in Paris are not always genuine gargoyles – many of them are guardian spirits or even esoteric symbols.

The head of the demon Medusa, with her hair of intertwined snakes, is an armrest for a gigantic statue of Leonardo da Vinci, at Amboise on the banks of the Loire.

DEMONIC HEADS

Germany has a great many demonic heads, often on buildings of special esoteric significance. For example, in the two German cities which are associated with the worst excesses of the witchcraft craze, Bamberg and Würzburg, there are a great range of demonic heads on the medieval buildings which are linked with the persecutions. In Bamberg, the gateway leading into the old *Residenz* of the Bishop, the centre for witchcraft persecution in the city, is decorated with a central demonic head which looks suspiciously like a satanic mask. In Würzburg the Ratskeller, which was formerly the administrative centre for the witch-hunters, has similar decorations, and the adjacent building has a large collection of satanic masks. Many German cathedrals possess excellent collections of demonic gargoyles, of which the best are probably those at Worms. Also at Worms cathedral in the tympanum which shows the miracles worked by St Nicholas, there is a fine image of a demon who is raising a storm at sea.

In England, the demonic tradition is found at its best in the gargoyles on cathedrals and churches, and there are few cities and towns which cannot boast a good collection of such demon lore. At opposite ends of the architectural scale, fine examples are found

The demonic head at the centre of the arch leading into the old administrative buildings at the Bishop's *Residenz*, in Bamberg, is an outer indication of the dark deeds which were carried out there during the excesses of the witch-hunts.

The external fabric of the cathedral at Worms has many impressive demons and grotesque gargoyles. One of the most interesting shows a demon attempting to cause a shipwreck. In medieval times it was widely believed that all storms (and calms) were brought about by demons or witches, who had power over the winds and waves.

Many people believe that the many demons among the flying buttresses of the cathedral of St John at s'Hertogenbosch, in Holland, influenced the infernal imagery of the city's greatest son, the painter Hieronymus Bosch.

on such very different buildings as Manchester Cathedral and the parish church at Littleborough in Lancashire, where the cat-faced gargoyles are particularly unusual in having esoteric sigils incised upon their sides.

Spain has a fine range of gargoyles in the demonic tradition, especially in Palma de Mallorca, but the pride of Spain in the diabolic field is without doubt the paintings by Hieronymus Bosch in the Prado, Madrid. It is not surprising to learn that at least one art historian has suggested that Bosch derived his interest in demons from his acquaintance with the gargoyles on the cathedral of St John, in s'Hertogenbosch, his birthplace in Holland. The 96 statues – most of them of a demonic nature – which tangle the superb flying buttresses of the cathedral were there long before he was born, and in some cases their forms seem to presage the horrifying monsters which appear in his mysterious pictures.

Manchester cathedral is filled with esoteric images, many of them derived from early Christian tradition. Inside the building, a host of gilded angels appear to hang in space, while on the outer fabric, very material and corporeal demons seem to mock the world beyond.

GOYA'S PAINTINGS OF WITCHES

Spain had an important painter who rivalled Bosch in satire, if not in exuberance of theme – this was Goya, whose interest in witchcraft led him to etch and paint many scenes of demonism and witches, theoretically almost stamped out in Spain by the Inquisition. Goya's country house, La Quinta del Sordo (The Deaf Man's House – so named, it would appear, long before Goya bought it, though the artist suffered terribly from deafness) on the bank of the Manzanares near Madrid, was filled with a series of 'Black Paintings' – frescoes dealing with dark subjects. The majority (including the terrible *Saturn Devouring his Children*) he later translated onto canvas, and they now hang in the Prado, Madrid. A memorial to Goya's genius stands outside the main entrance of the Prado. This is a bas-relief of the naked *Maja*, once thought to be a portrait of the Duchess of Alba (the original painting of which hangs in the Prado), with a number of grotesque faces and demons hovering in the astral space above. These demons are a sly commentary on the Pandora's box which may be opened in the mind of a man when confronted with the naked body of a lovely woman. Goya was the Spanish painter *par excellence*, yet he died in exile, in the French town of Bordeaux.

Goya's most remarkable demonic pictures usually deal with witchcraft themes, and the finest of the surviving series are from six canvases commissioned by the wealthy Duchess of Osuna. Among them is *The Devil's Lamp*, now in the National Gallery, London, with a theme based on a satirical play of the same name with which Goya was familiar. The frightened man in the picture believes that he is in the room of a witch, and is convinced that his own life will be snuffed out if the wick in the lamp held by the demonic goat is extinguished. This explains why he is attempting to replenish the oil, even as the wick burns. A second picture with a related theme from this series is *The Witches' Sabbath*, now in the Museo Lázaro Galdiano in Madrid. It shows women offering their children (in various states of starvation) to the horned Devil.

As well as the works of Bosch and Goya, there are a vast number of other demon images in public galleries throughout Europe. One of the most compelling is the painting by the Italian Michael Pacher, now in the Alte Pinakothek, Munich: it shows the Devil, completely under the control of St Wolfgang, being forced to hold the missal

The curious modern memorial to Goya, outside the main entrance to the Prado in Madrid, symbolises the world of demonic dreams.

from which the saint reads. The theme of the Devil being dominated is uncommon: a much more popular theme is that of the magician who has raised the devil and finds him far more difficult to control than he had originally foreseen.

The engravings of Cock, based on the drawings of Brueghel the Elder, touch on many occult themes, but the most interesting are those linked with the literature of demonology, which seems to have occupied Brueghel's imagination almost as much as it did that of Bosch. The theme of the temptation of St Anthony has always been popular with artists because of the opportunity it gives them to call up a nightmare world from the infernal regions. Jacques Callot favoured this theme, and his very convincing demons have appeared in many witchcraft texts. Callot was born at Nancy in 1592 and died there at the age of 45. For all his fame, he was something of an itinerant, and travelled widely throughout Europe, making sketches of unusual and occult subjects. He witnessed the siege of Breda, and made a series of engravings of what he had seen, and followed this with pictures of the sieges of the Ile de Ré and La Rochelle. In his studies of the invasion of Lorraine by Louis XIII's soldiers, which resulted in the series *Miseries of War*, 1633, he anticipated Goya by almost 200 years in depicting the horrors of war with terrifying accuracy.

This engraving by Cock, after a drawing by Breughel the Elder, portraying the demons of hell torturing their victims, is typical of the period.

The power of the saints is often overlooked by demonologists – here, however, we have a portrayal of the superior spiritual power of St Wolfgang who, with the sign of the cross, reduces the hideous demon to the role of lectern, outside the church. Panel by Michael Pacher, *c.* 1483. Kunsthistorisches Museum, Vienna.

BENVENUTO CELLINI RAISES DEMONS IN ROME

The demons of Europe are found not only in sculpture and pictures, but also in literature, and many hundreds of books (especially those derived from medieval sources) give accounts of actual or imagined encounters with demons in various parts of Europe. In his extraordinary autobiography Benvenuto Cellini, the Italian artist and silversmith, recounts an adventure he had with a friend Vincenzio Romoli, and a priest, in the Colosseum at Rome. The priest, who was intimately familiar with the black arts, had persuaded Cellini that he would be able to ask demons to help him find his lost mistress Angelica, and this was sufficient to induce the artist to meddle in the forbidden realm. The small group waited in the Colosseum until nightfall, then the priest, in necromancer's robes, drew the conjuration circle in the earth of the arena, and carried out a number of rites with perfumes, fire and an evil-smelling substance. After an hour or so of these incantations more and more demons appeared until, as Cellini records, 'the Colosseum was full of devils'. Since information about Angelica was not forthcoming, the priest said that they would have to return on the following night, bringing with them a little boy of pure virginity. Cellini returned with one of his twelve-year-old assistants, and after similar ceremonies to the previous evening, the priestly necromancer called again on the legions, and 'in a short space of time the whole Colosseum was full of a hundredfold as hideous as any as had appeared upon the first occasion'. This time, Cellini was able to ask the question about his missing Angelica, and the demons told him when he would see her again. After experiencing the terrifying appearance of so many monstrous creatures that they almost gave themselves up for dead, the conjuration ended with the first light of morning. Long after the four had left the Colosseum, however, the young assistant claimed that he could still see demons 'skipping now along the roofs and now upon the ground'. In Naples, on the precise day that the demons had prophesied, Cellini found Angelica, and the couple were passionately reunited.

Jacques Callot, whose pen-drawing was the basis for this magnificent demon-head, from his *Temptation of St Anthony* series, had a profound interest in demonic lore, and has left very many drawings and engravings of arcane, occult and demonological subjects.

Frankenstein, as much as his monstrous creation, was a literary invention, a product of Mary Shelley's fertile mind, but a more recent book entitled *The Frankenstein Diaries*, by Hubert Venables, has given the invention a home as well as a name. This nineteenth-century engraving is said to represent Schwarzstein Castle, the ancestral home of the Frankensteins.

FRANKENSTEIN AND THE CONJURATION OF DEMONS

The modern notion of the creation of Frankenstein is really little more than a development of the old 'conjuration of demons' theme in literature. However, instead of standing in a magical circle and evoking the presence of demons which, as we have seen, could so often get out of control, Frankenstein actually builds his own, and finds to his horror that he has little or no power over it.

A nineteenth-century engraving of Schwarzstein Castle, described as the home of the Frankenstein family, is a delightful piece of romantic invention, yet the story of Frankenstein began in a place in Switzerland which was real enough. In 1881, Mary Shelley, her husband the poet, and Lord Byron spent part of a wet summer in Montalegre, near Lake Leman in Switzerland, reading and writing ghost stories. From this endeavour emerged Mary Shelley's classic *Frankenstein, or the Modern Prometheus*, which tells the tale of a student from Geneva who learns the terrible secret of how to give life to inanimate matter. With bones collected from burial places, dissecting rooms and charnel houses, he constructs a hybrid human, and charges it with life. The monster is filled with murderous hate, and kills the bride of its creator. Frankenstein undertakes a perilous trip to slay the monster, but dies in the attempt: soon afterwards, the monster commits suicide. The fascinating *Frankenstein Diaries*, 'translated and edited' (i.e. written) by Hubert Venables, contains many interesting diagrams of the 'experiments'

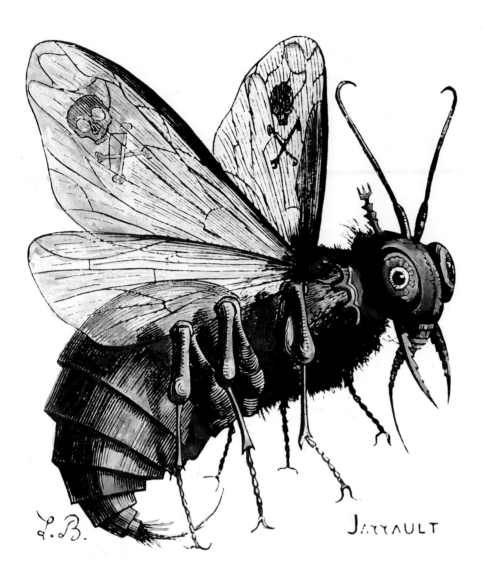

The famous image of Beelzebub in his guise of the Lord of the Flies is a nineteenth-century invention. The French journalist, Collin de Plancy, created this image to illustrate his encyclopedia of demonic beings.

A print published by Witkowski in his work *L'Art Profane à l'Eglise*, 1908, showing St John baptising the Magdalen.

Drawing after a relief on the façade of Ste-Croix, Bordeaux, showing a woman being punished by a demon and his serpents for indulging in the sin of lust. The three drawings of this page and the two on the opposite page are all from Witowski's *L'Art Profane à l'Eglise*, 1908.

leading up to the creation of the monster, and locates the home of the 'modern Prometheus' in the gloomy forest of Schwarzstein.

Undoubtedly the most famous of all nineteenth-century demon-books is that written by the journalist and occultist Jacques Albin Simon Collin, who adopted as a pseudonym the name of his birthplace, Plancy. Under the name Collin de Plancy, he published a collection of the most popular demonic legends of Europe (not a few of which were invented by de Plancy himself), which were illustrated with engravings. His image of Beelzebub, in his character of 'Lord of the Flies', with a skull and crossbones emblazoned on each of his wings, has become one of the standard representations of this demon.

Perhaps the most remarkable book to deal with demonic, profane, and occult art in European churches and cathedrals is *L'Art Profane à l'Eglise* (1908) by G. J. Witkowski, which contains a large number of engravings revealing the surprising variety of these images. For all the stark demonology in his collection of illustrations, Witkowski's selection is not without its humour: for example, he reproduces an amusing drawing from a manuscript in the Bibliothèque Nationale in Paris, showing St John baptising the Magdalen, who is naked. Outside the church seven men (no doubt representative of the seven planetary types) attempt to peer through holes in the door to see the naked woman. It can almost be described as a medieval version of the theme set out in the later Goya memorial outside the Prado in Madrid.

The theme of Lust as its own punishment is sometimes found in the medieval image of a woman having her breasts sucked by a pair of toads or snakes; there are two fine examples in the church of Notre-Dame at Montmorillon in France, and another on the façade of the central arch of the church of Ste Croix in Bordeaux, which also contains some of the most original zodiacal images in the country. In the cathedral at Basle there is a colossal statue said to represent Lust, one of the original seven deadly sins, represented in this case by a libertine who is making eyes at a young woman. The slit down the back of his gown shows that his flesh is being devoured by snakes and toads, while his lower parts are being burned by flames issuing from the mouth of a devil, who emerges from the ground behind him. This is medieval symbolism showing that the inner appetites of men are themselves caused by demonic activity, and should be resisted. From St-Pierre at Moissac, Witkowski reproduces a drawing of the famous medieval carving on the south wall of the abbey-church, depicting much the same theme; in this case, the woman who has sinned is attacked by a demon with snakes and

Right: drawing based on a sculptural relief of the façade of St Pierre, Moissac, showing the hellish punishments meted out to a woman who indulged in the sin of lust. Her punishment included having serpents suck at her breasts, and a huge toad gnaw at her private parts.

Far right: drawing based on sculpted reliefs in St Pierre, Moissac, showing demons riding the backs of an evil wealthy man (right) and an avaricious man (left), revealing the ease with which demons may 'possess' such men of weak character.

toads in a way which, Witkowski admits, makes one's hair stand on end with horror. In the same church, we find a carving said to illustrate the parable of the wicked rich man and the avaricious man: horned devils are riding on the shoulders of the men, showing their diabolical domination over these humans. However, Witkowski appears to have missed the most intriguing of the Moissac demons, for he makes no mention of the capital in the cloisters, which portrays huge-headed demons pulling at some instrument of torture. Witkowski does however illustrate an enigmatic figure in the cathedral at Fribourg: on the abacus of a capital there is a nereid feeding a fish-baby, who holds in his left hand a bird and his own private parts. This symbolism defies explanation, in much the same way as the demons on the capital at Moissac.

Above right: this drawing of a sculpture on a capital in Fribourg cathedral is one of the most puzzling of medieval images. The nereid nursing a fish-child may well be an esoteric reference to the Virgin Mary with the child Jesus (later to become the fisher of men, linked with the Age of Pisces) as half-fish, half-child. The bird in his hand would therefore represent the human soul, given over to his care.

Above left: Death and the Doctor. Drawing of a fresco of the *Dance of Death* in the church of St Jean, Basle.

An image of a monstrous demon on one of the capitals in the cloisters at St Pierre, Moissac. Several of the capitals in these cloisters are esoteric or occult.

FAUST, THE GERMAN LEGEND

The legend of Faust is steeped in ancient mythology, yet for many years it has been hung, albatross-like, around the neck of a real historical figure named Faustus (or Fust) who lived in south-western Germany. This link appears to have been made by Johann Gast, a Protestant priest, who claimed to have met Faust personally, and later preached a sermon about his supposed magical and supernatural abilities, thus helping to lay the foundations of the legends. Some time later Gast wrote the first of many literary works to deal with the Faustian mythology, the *Faustbuch* (1587). This text, which many believed to be a historical biography, is partly a work of the imagination and partly a collection of stories and legends about Faust and other magicians, culled from many sources, and it has provided much material for artists, writers and poets to exercise their imaginations. Even if Faust never existed, history would have had to invent him, because he is a manifestation of the distinctive human urge to live now and pay later. The fact that Faustus, the magician, almost certainly had no existence outside the mind of man, has not prevented some towns and cities from claiming him as their own. For example, Knittlingen in Germany claims to be his birthplace, and has converted its ancient Rathaus into a Faust Museum. In Leipzig, in East Germany, there is a famous cellar-tavern, still used as a restaurant and bar, which is reputed to be the place where Faust and Mephistopheles drank.

Historians always seem anxious to pin the character of Faust on to a real person, and one theory claims that the original Faust was Johann Fust, the wealthy financier who backed the printer Gutenberg, and, in default of a loan, seized the printer's business, using the type and press to establish a new printing works of his own. This is hardly the stuff of demonic legend, and one suspects that associations between Fust and Faust rest more on the name than on any historical evidence. There is something significant in this ascription, however, for it was widely believed during the fifteenth century that the new art of printing was an invention of the Devil, and those who served the press where in thraldom to his Satanic Majesty.

The playwright, Christopher Marlowe, believed that his own work *The Tragicall History of Dr Faustus*, published in 1604, was based on the true life story of a Johann Faustus, a magician and astrologer who was born in Wurtemberg in the fifteenth

This crude woodcut, from the title page of Christopher Marlowe's play *The Tragicall History of Doctor Faustus*, 1604, portrays both scholar and devil in garish, almost melodramatic terms.

century. However, the legends of Faust with which Marlowe was familiar were derived from a book which described him as a 'notorious magician' and a 'Master of the Black Art', which was published in 1587 in Frankfurt am Main only two years before Marlowe wrote his play.

Whatever its true historical origin, the theme of the Faust legend is very ancient, and is rooted in the notion of a pact with the devil. In the oldest versions of the story, in return for an additional 24 years (the period varies from story to story), Faust agrees to bequeath his soul to the Devil. The Devil insists that this agreement must be recorded in a document, signed – if not actually drawn up – in Faust's own blood. In essence, the Devil keeps his bargain, and most of the story, at least in European literature, consists of the picaresque adventures, with scurrilous and sexual undertones, of a man offered unbridled pleasure. It is the ending, with Faust's realisation that all the pleasures in the world are not worth the loss of his soul and the prospect of spending eternity in Hell, which turn what is essentially a racy adventure story into a tragedy.

Poets and dramatists were eager to develop all the implications of this tale, in which they traced the medieval theme of Everyman assailed by his own inner voices. Although no less a genius than Rembrandt made an etching of the Faust theme, in which he portrayed the magician in his study before being tempted by Mephistopheles, the true romantic imagery of the story was not explored fully until Goethe tackled the theme. The genius of this man transformed what was little more than a fairly pedestrian piece of grimoire literature (save in Marlowe's rendering) into art of the highest calibre, linking Faust's damnation to a spiritual concept which, even today, is frequently overlooked by commentators. In Goethe's version the temptation of Faust is prefaced by a scene in which the Devil obtains permission from God to attempt the ruination of Faust: this harks back to medieval demonological lore, which insisted that demons could only work their evil 'with the permission of God' who was Master over all. We are then presented with an insight into the soul of Faust who, for all his mastery of magical lore, is disillusioned and in a state of despair – the very image of modern Man. Faust is, in brief, ready for temptation and for an extension of life-experiences on a different plane of being; he, like modern Man (to take the analogy further), therefore makes a good subject for Mephistopheles, who insists that the agreement drawn up between them be written in that very special liquid, human blood. Here again, as we shall see, the notion of a bloody pact merely follows the demonological tradition.

In Goethe's version, Faust recognises that if in the course of his self-indulgent progress through life he were ever to find a moment of enjoyment so seductive that he called out to Mephistopheles to stop the flow of time, then he truly would be damned. This philosophical Faust sees, indeed, that the modern tragedy of Man is somehow involved with the nature of his experience of reality, and with the passage of time itself.

Delacroix illustrated several scenes from Goethe's *Faust* using the new art of lithography; one of the most interesting image is that portraying the flight of Mephistopheles over a German city, which is almost certainly Leipzig.

According to the esotericist, Rudolf Steiner, Goethe's *Faust* was partially based on Paracelsus, the sixteenth-century occultist. Paracelsus was born at Etzel, near Einsiedeln, now in Switzerland, in 1493, and after qualifying as a doctor adopted a wandering style of life which took him through many parts of Europe; he has left behind a trail of legends and historical truths. He studied astrology, alchemy and the cabbala, and there is some indication that he was also one of the early Rosicrucians who worked in Europe long before the earliest Rosy-Cross documents were published (see chapter 5). As with so many men of genius, he was frequently persecuted, yet the rich corpus of his writings show that he was one of the greatest occultists of all time. The fact that he was a practising occultist who was fundamentally misunderstood by his contemporaries is one of the reasons why Steiner recognises him as an historical source for some of Goethe's insights into the Faust legend.

The notion of the pact was of considerable importance in the established legal view of witchcraft in late medieval Germany. It has been described by the historian of the dark art, Rossell Hope Robbins, as 'the very essence of witchcraft', on the grounds that an agreement with the Devil, whether in writing or the spoken word, was rank opposition to God and a denial of the agreement implicit in baptism. Most legal experts

Mephistopheles. One of Eugene Delacroix's series of black and white lithographs illustrating Goethe's *Faust*.

believed that it was the act of the pact, rather than any subsequent act of evil-working, which rendered a witch susceptible to arrest, condemnation and death.

One of the most popular legends about the demonic pact in medieval literature, which has been incorporated into the tale of Faust, has an ancestry which goes back at least to the sixth century. This story tells how Theophilus, deprived of his ecclesiastical post, sold his soul to the Devil in order to recover his position. The tale of this encounter is illustrated by what is probably the only carving of a demon-pact in existence. It can be seen at the abbey church of Souillac in France. In this impressive carving we see the conjurer Salatin handing over the signed pact to the Devil, who claims Theophilus. At the top of the carving, as the deal is being concluded with the death of the ecclesiastic, the Virgin Mary steals the pact from the Devil's hands. The wording of the pact, as preserved in a dramatic version entitled *Le Miracle de Theophile*, records that the formula was written in human blood, the paper sealed with the Devil's personal ring. While the Souillac image may well be a unique stone carving, the story of Theophilus and his pact was popular in medieval times, and several manuscripts depicting the infamous paper can be found in museums.

While relatively few formal demonic pacts have survived the holocaust days of medieval witchcraft, an interesting collection of demonic parchments, including a few pacts, is preserved in the Bibliothèque Nationale, in Paris. Before glancing at one or two of these, it is important to bear in mind that in medieval times there was a widespread belief that while witches and magicians undoubtedly did sign pacts, there was really no need for such a document, as making a verbal agreement to work as a witch was sufficient. The pact therefore was essentially an invisible undertaking, in which the prospective witch would renounce Christ, his faith, baptism and the Catholic Church, and then enact some ritual to show his new allegiance to the Devil, such as the drinking

This huge programme from the abbey church at Souillac is probably the only medieval image showing the story of a demonic pact in sculpture. In the centre Salatin presents the Devil with the signed pact. At the side, the same Devil claims the soul of Theophilus. The situation is saved by the Virgin Mary (above) who snatches the pact away from the Devil.

A menacing demon presents the demonic pact to Theophilus, in this early thirteenth-century illumination from the *Psalter of Queen Ingeborg of Denmark*, now in the Musée Condé, Chantilly.

of the blood of a murdered child. 'This done', wrote Johannes Nider in 1435, 'he [the new witch] forthwith takes himself to conceive and hold within himself an image of our art and the chief rules of this sect'. In later times, this ritual of making a pact became more complex in the eyes of the witch hunters, and horrid praxes of a highly imaginative kind were introduced into the rituals, such as the kissing of the posterior of the Devil by the new witch, and submitting to the sexual embrace of the Devil or his minions. The sexual element implicit in the agreement of a woman to serve the Devil became one of the most popular themes in the iconography of witchcraft, permitting one of the few 'official' vehicles for salacious imagery in popular art. Perhaps it was all fantasy, yet many people suffered because of it: in 1453, for example, at Évreux, the prior of St-Germain-en-Laye was sentenced to perpetual imprisonment for having intercourse with a demon, for flying on a broomstick, and for kissing a goat under its tail.

In 1626, when Guazzo of Milan wrote his influential book on witchcraft, he provided numerous crude woodcuts which show very many stages in the solemn pact which simply had not existed in the simpler days of Faust. These include images showing the rebaptizing of the witch in the name of the Devil, the Devil's confirmation of the new initiate by scratching with his claws on the forehead of the witch to erase spiritually the baptismal mark of the water, the image of the Devil striking out the name of the new witch from the Book of Life and entering it in his own Book of Death, and the promise of the witch to kill children by black magic or to suck the blood of children.

In the fascinating Musée Basque at Bayonne there is a small collection of paintings in a room which is sometimes (rather ambitiously) described as a witchcraft museum. This series of pictures by Jose de Pena illustrates the story of local witches and their sabbats as revealed during the interrogations by a Royal Commission presided over by Pierre de Lancre in 1609. De Lancre left records of these 'trials', as well as a number of interesting engravings which illustrate his book. Not all these paintings relate to Bayonne, however: one, depicting witches baptising toads, is sited in the cemetery of St Jean-de-Luz, while another shows the Devil confronting de Lancre himself in the Maison Belsarenea at St-Pée-sur-Nivelle. Another picture shows an important sabbat,

A witch preparing to fly to a sabbat; a drawing by Jose de Pena, the basis for one of the frescoes in the witchcraft section of the Musée Basque in Bayonne.

A highly imaginative coloured engraving showing one of the many sabbats held near Bayonne in the early seventeenth century.

said to have been held near Biarritz, while another is shown on the top of the mountain of La Rhune. One interesting belief established by the Royal Commission (and recorded in these paintings) is that demons from India and Japan, who had been chased from their native lands by the European missionaries, chose to settle in France. As a result English and Scottish travellers, who had come to Bordeaux to buy wines, had 'seen great hordes of demons in terrible human form passing through France'. These demons apparently chose to settle in the area south of Bayonne, thus accounting for the rapid spread of witchcraft among the Basques.

The tragic history of witchraft in Europe has left its distinctive mark on many cities and villages, and there is scarcely a museum which does not contain witch-bottles, poppets, spells, instruments of torture, and other grisly remains of the earliest of our holocausts, even if these are not always on display. Not all historical remains are still recognised as such: for example, how many visitors to the church in Mora, in Sweden, realise that 15 children, found guilty of witchcraft, were executed near this building, and a further 36 were condemned to be whipped outside its doorways every Sunday for a year? And how many visitors to the numerous delightful towns and cities of Germany and France suspect the dark secrets hidden in the fifteenth- and sixteenth-century buildings in such charming places as Strasbourg, Metz and Breslau, and in the fascinating medieval cities of Bamberg and Würzburg? In fact, these last two were at one time the most notorious centres of witchcraft in Germany, for reasons which are a perpetual disgrace to the medieval legal system and the Jesuits, who appear to have started and supported the witch-hunts in these cities.

The town on the horizon of this demon-haunted witch-burning is probably Mora, in Sweden, for the engraving illustrates the burning of witches near there in 1670.

THE WITCH-HUNTING CRAZE

These dreadful stories are a reminder that the pact, upon which so much of the medieval notion of witchcraft was based, was largely a bureaucratic invention of the church. The disease of witchcraft was in many respects an invention of those who should have been an inspiration to the people rather than their destroyers. Demonic pacts may have been relatively rare, yet the Spaniards had accused Sixtus V of selling his soul to the Devil in order to become Pope – and it was, indeed, a Pope who was the first openly to encourage the prosecution of witches and to lay down the guidelines for the pursuit of this heresy in the following centuries. Pope John XXII, no doubt concerned about the spread of the old heresies in Carcassonne (see page 11), commanded the Inquisition to take action against all those who practised magical and diabolical arts, and to confiscate their properties. It was this last idea – that an accuser might gain financially from hunting out witches – that really boosted the growth of the witch-hunt, for it gave an incentive to people in positions of power to seek out witches even among innocent people.

The fact that Bamberg and Würzburg have been credited with the most terrible of all stories about the witch-hunting craze seems to have arisen because of the social conditions which existed in the late medieval period. Both these towns, with the villages in the surrounding countryside, were virtual city-states, ruled by Prince-Bishops, who had almost absolute power which they all too frequently misused. This misuse of their power led to the infamous witchcraft craze, which is now recorded only in one or two old prints and in the histories of two or three buildings in these cities.

A rare print of the Bamberg 'witch house' – which is now called the *Hexenhaus* but was originally known as the *Malefitz Haus*, from a Germanic-Latin term for witchcraft –

An engraving of the infamous
Hexenhaus at Bamberg, built by
the Prince-Bishop Johann Georg II
Fuchs von Dornheim, in 1627, both
as a prison and a place of torture
for suspected witches.

Below left: one of the most painful
of the frequently used tortures was
strappado. The hands of the victim
were tied behind his back and he
was hoisted by his hands into the
air (sometimes with weights
attached to his feet). On the release
of a winch, the weighted body
dropped and the arms of the victim
were dislocated at the shoulders.

Below right: a selection of
instruments of torture, from a
woodcut, *c.* 1513. Of all these, the
most terrible was the wheel
(middle left) upon which the bones
of the body were broken.

is frequently reproduced in historical accounts of witchcraft. It was built in 1627 by the
Prince-Bishop of Bamberg, Johann Georg II Fuchs von Dornheim, and was especially
designed to deal with the victims of the witch-hunts, with rooms set aside as prison cells
and a number of well-appointed torture chambers. The instruments of torture within
this building (and several other towns and villages had similar *Hexenhäuser*) included
thumbscrews, leg-vices, instruments for strappado, friction collars, scalding-baths,
instruments for tearing off women's breasts, and a horrible collection of knives and
gouges.

The Prince-Bishop of Bamberg, who bore the dubious title of *Hexenbischof* (witch-
bishop), is said to have burned over 600 victims. The year 1627, when the print
illustrated above was made, was a particularly dreadful year, for not only were several
hundreds of suspects arrested and burned, but even the Vice-Chancellor of Bamberg, Dr

George Haan, who had made some effort to restrict the mania, was arrested. In the following year, in spite of an Imperial order to the contrary, Haan and his wife and daughter were burned alive, his supposed crimes hingeing on the notion that he was a witch-lover. The cause of the holocaust in Bamberg, which claimed many thousands of innocent victims, was essentially financial, as it was in many other European towns. The property of all those condemned was forfeit to the Prince-Bishops who, as a result of the persecutions, became very wealthy men, at the head of vast bureaucracies concerned only with arresting, burning and the confiscation of the local people's property.

The inhabitants of Bamberg have made an understandable effort to delete this terrible period from their history – the 'witch house' has been pulled down, and now there are no books dealing with the witch-hunting to be found in their public libraries. The only tangible remains of the *hexen* are in the State Library, which houses a collection of Latin manuscripts relating to the trials. One piece of architecture will remind the specialist of the cruel times, however, for the beautiful building in the cathedral square, which is now a museum, was once the Prince-Bishop's administrative centre, from where the vast bureaucracy involved in bringing so many people to their deaths was run.

The persecutions in Würzburg arose from similar financial considerations as at Bamberg, though in this case the rapacious Prince-Bishop was Phillip Adolf von Ehrenberg who is reputed to have burned over 900 victims. It would certainly be misleading to call them witches: many were young children, some of whom showed exceptional courage. For example, the schoolboy Philip Schuck was still denying all charges even after he had been savagely lashed with a rawhide 46 times, but after a further 77 lashes (the flogging could have gone on indefinitely) he confessed to being a witch, and named several accomplices. Like all the other child victims, some of them little more than seven years old, he was executed.

The old administrative centre of the Bishop's *Residenz* in Bamberg, part of which is now a museum. In the seventeenth century, during the height of the witch-hunts, the building was the bureaucratic centre of the purges. In modern times it is one of the most lovely of the many surviving medieval buildings, but all associations with witchcraft have been forgotten.

Würzburg Castle, the fortress in
which many suspects were confined
during the infamous purges, when
over 900 people were condemned
to the stake as witches.

Again, in modern times, there appears to have been a sort of conspiracy of silence concerning this awful period. One official guide in Würzburg recently affirmed that Würzburg had never seen the excesses of other cities (such as Bamberg) during the witch-hunting period, and that so far as she knew only one person convicted of witchcraft in the city was executed. As at Bamberg, very little tangible evidence remains of the 900 deaths – the Bishop's residence, from which the witch trials were directed has been pulled down and replaced by an elegant mansion, designed by Balthasar Neumann, and set in superb gardens. It is as though nothing terrible could have happened in this town, yet across the river is the fortress of Marienberg which was the fortified home of the Prince-Bishop during the witch-hunts and, for all its gaunt beauty, a visible reminder of the terrible past.

Other centres where the witch-hunts followed similar lines were Treves, Strasbourg, Breslau and Fulda, yet in truth it is likely that there is not a single village or town in Europe which did not lose one or more of its inhabitants to the mania against witches during the sixteenth and seventeenth centuries.

Although there was no legal need for a documentary pact, some have survived, and the historian, Robbins, has reproduced several in his book, *The Encyclopedia of Witchcraft and Demonology*. They include a highly imaginative promissory note signed in 1676 by a nobleman in Pignerole. Among other things it required an initial down payment of £100,000 in gold, and regular monthly payments of £1,000: at this time £50 would buy a comfortable house. As a cautionary note, the pact has a clause which asserts that the 'foresaid gold must not be false, must not disappear in one's hand, or turn to stone or coals. It should be metal stamped by the hands of men, legal and valid in all lands.' On the strength of this document (which was to remain valid for 50 years, and ensured fame, fortune and women for the signatory), the nobleman was convicted and died in prison long before the pact was concluded.

URBAIN GRANDIER, CORRUPTION AT LOUDUN

Almost certainly the most famous pact is the one introduced as evidence at the trial of Urbain Grandier at Loudun, in 1634. It is written in looking-glass Latin, in confirmation of the widespread belief that demons did everything in reverse to show their contempt for Christianity. The agreement is signed by Satanas, Beelzebub, Lucifer, Elimi, Leviathan and Astaroth, in some cases with their own distinctive sigils. The Latin is bad, and savours more of a seventeenth-century style than the medieval one generally associated with demons. (Perhaps the demonic scribes, like C. S. Lewis's modern Screwtape, constantly refine and update their calligraphy and literary style in order to move with the times?) The pact is only one of several relating to the Loudun case. Preserved in the Bibliothèque Nationale in Paris is a manuscript autograph undertaking, dated 19 May 1625 and signed by the demon Asmodeus, who promises to quit the body of one of the demoniac Loudun nuns. This undertaking (which, of course, is not a pact) was forced upon the demon by Jean Baptiste Gault, one of those in charge of exorcising the nuns. This demon, along with a number of others, undertakes to escape the body of the nun by making a slit the length of a pin below her heart, and then through her chemise, bodice and cassock, through which he might squeeze. This surgical approach appears to be just one more example of the demon's terror over his charge, for in other cases of exorcism the Devil has no difficulty in escaping through the mouth, or other natural orifices.

Grandier is famous for more than merely the survival of this patent forgery of a pact. His story is still remembered in the medieval walled town of Loudun, which now has an old-world charm and sleepiness which it most certainly did not have in the seventeenth century, when it was an important regional centre.

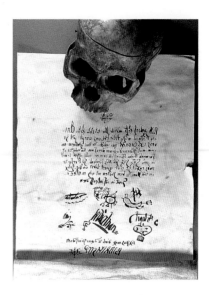

This Latin pact, written in reversed Latin, is signed in mirror-writing by a host of demons. The original, now in the Bibliothèque Nationale, in Paris, is one of several pacts relating to the trial and burning of Urbain Grandier at Loudun in 1634.

The Porte du Martray, which leads into Loudun, and to the square of St-Pierre-du-Marché, where Urbain Grandier was burned to death.

Grandier was a parish priest of St Pierre-du-Marché whose luxurious lifestyle and philandering had earned him the dislike of various local men of influence. Not that Grandier's behaviour was excessive by the standards of the day, when the Church was regarded as a career rather than a calling by many well-educated young men. But Grandier took less care than most to conceal his activities, which attracted first envy and then hatred as several daughters of important local families allowed themselves to be seduced by him. He was eventually charged with immorality by one of his numerous enemies, the Bishop of Poitiers, and although he was found guilty, his influence was such that he was able to get his sentence of suspension from clerical duties lifted after only one year.

Urban Grandier's enemies then decided to use the all-powerful witchcraft laws to put an end to him. Their plot was advanced (perhaps even suggested) by an outbreak of 'demonic possession' at the Ursuline convent in Loudun. Such incidents were not uncommon and although we would explain them now as sexual hysteria, in the seventeenth century Satan was to blame. And since Satan needed an agent or witch to carry out his infernal work, who better to blame than Grandier? As the glamorous and handsome seducer probably featured in the fantasies of the disturbed women already, and the name of their confessor was mentioned in their demented outpourings, what more proof was needed? So perfect was the case against the unfortunate Grandier – the only truly devilish thing in the whole affair – it is surprising that the first attempt to put this plan into operation came to nothing. It was only when an influential friend of Cardinal Richelieu's came to Loudun that Grandier's enemies sensed a real chance of such a plan working. The nuns, apparently aided by some of Grandier's discarded mistresses, conspired to charge him with acts of adultery, incest and sacrilege – acts, they claimed, which had taken place even within the walls of the church itself. He was imprisoned on 30 November 1633 at Angers, where his jailors claimed to have found the insensitive devil's marks on his private parts, though two doctors later testified that no such marks existed.

Grandier's trial is one of the most corrupt in the history of French witchcraft, for he was not permitted to be tried in a secular court, and normal legal procedure was ignored. The absurd mirror-written pact described above was produced and accepted as evidence: conscience-stricken nuns who sought to recant their charges and were anxious to tell the truth about the matter, were forbidden to speak, while Grandier's friends were not allowed to appear in his defence. Needless to say, Grandier was found guilty of witchcraft, and sentenced to be tortured and burned. The hideous torture, designed to make him reveal accomplices, was so extreme that the marrow squirted from his broken bones. With exceptional bravery Urbain Grandier refused to name any others, or even to denounce those who had ensnared him. The profligate priest more than redeemed himself by the quiet dignity with which he suffered both his torment and his death.

St Pierre-du-Marché, where he was compelled to kneel as a broken man before execution, is no longer used as a church, but the market place opposite, where he was burned alive, is now a delightful square, with simple façades which must surely have looked down upon his cruel end. The medieval gateway now called the Porte du Martray leads into a street which must have had much the same appearance in Grandier's time, and the curious gargoyles on the walls of St Hilaire are the very ones which looked down at the events of the seventeenth century.

The sequel to this sorry tale is reminiscent of a gothic horror story. The man who lit the pyre on which Grandier was burned was dead within the month, his last words being guilty ramblings about Grandier's death. The man who claimed to have found the devil's marks on Grandier's private parts died in insane delirium. One of the other priests was banished in 1640 for his collusion in the matter of the demonic nuns, who, for some years after the execution, continued to exhibit themselves (naturally for a fee) in convulsions and lewd positions, thereby providing a good source of income for their nunnery.

Among the collection of demon-scribed manuscripts in Paris is one 'signed' by a devil named Nephtali, who undertakes 'with great regret' to smash the church pulpit of the Vicar of Loudun and to carry it 'from that place by breaking a way through the roof

One of the impressive gargoyles in Loudun, on the church of St-Hilaire-du Matray. Grandier would have walked beneath this gargoyle whenever he went to his church in the square of St-Pierre-du-Marché.

thereof'. There is no record of whether this creature kept his promise, but the roof of the church is in a good state of repair, and the pulpit is still in place. As the judges at witchcraft trials were always at pains to point out – there was little point in anyone signing a pact for the Devil, being by nature a consummate liar, had no intention of keeping his word.

IMAGES OF WITCHCRAFT

It is undoubtedly the Walpurgis Night scenes in Goethe's *Faust* which did most to popularize the Brocken in the Harz Mountains as a witches' playground, yet it had been associated with witchcraft for many centuries before the play was written. Witches' sabbats were always reputed to take place in desolate or inaccessible areas to which the witches themselves might fly with ease, carrying their familiars with them. As Grillot de Givry admits, these accursed gatherings were supposed to take place among the menhirs on the heaths of Carnac, on the summit of the Blocksberg and – if the Abbé

Woodcut from the 1591 witchcraft pamphlet, *Newes from Scotlande, declaring the Damnable Life and death of Doctor Fian, a notable Sorcere who was burned at Edenbrough in January Last.* To the left, a black devil is preaching to the witches from the pulpit of the Old Kirk at North Berwick.

An engraving of a sabbat on the Brocken, which shows the mountain as a small hill, and illustrates most of the traditional activities of witches.

Thiers is to be believed – even on the summit of the Puy-de-Dome, in the Auvergne. The witches knew no limitations, and would even meet inside churches. They are said to have done this at the 'demoniac church' at Blokula in Sweden, while the witches of North Berwick in Scotland attended a sermon given by the Devil himself in the old church, which now stands deserted on the headland by the harbour. Of all these places, perhaps only the Blocksberg deserves its sinister reputation, though in relatively recent times it was the object of a calculated spoof by one of the great con men of modern psychism, Harry Price, who persuaded the philosopher C. E. M. Joad (amidst much media interest) to attempt the conjuration of spirits on the Brocken. The expedition was a fiasco, however.

The 25 pfenning ticket from Ilsenburg, near the witch-ridden Brocken, valid for 1921, sets out the popular notion of witchcraft to perfection. On the one side is the familiar witchcraft imagery of transvecting women, cauldrons, demons, owls and the like, while on the other side is the all-important Teutonic mythology, from which the tales of witchcraft originally emerged, to mingle with a different form of witchcraft born in ancient Greece and Rome.

A pre-War ticket to the Brocken from nearby Ilsenburg, price 25 pfennigs. The witchcraft imagery, albeit designed for modern popular taste, is in fact derived entirely from medieval superstitions and beliefs.

Since the Devil himself is frequently found in ecclesiastical sculptures, it is perhaps surprising that images of witches do not often appear on the walls of churches and cathedrals. A fine exception, however, is the quatrefoil, carved in the fourteenth century, on the western front of Lyons cathedral. It portrays a naked witch riding the Devil goat, her cloak streaming behind her to indicate that she is in full transvection, her right hand grasping (somewhat suggestively) at one of the goat's horns, and her left hand swinging what appears to be a cat, the most popular of all familiars.

JOAN OF ARC CHARGED WITH WITCHCRAFT

Undoubtedly the two most extraordinary French trials that used charges related to converse with demons and the actual invocation of demons as a means of attaining political ends were those of Joan of Arc and Gilles de Rais. Joan was burned in 1431, but was later vindicated and became the French heroine *par excellence*, while Gilles de Rais, who was hanged in 1440, is remembered now, thanks to Perrault, as the Bluebeard of fairytale.

In fact, although charges of witchcraft were included in the original indictments, Joan was not actually condemned as a witch, as is so often believed, but as a heretic. Long after her death she was rehabilitated, and canonized in 1920. Her statue, more often than not portraying her in male armour, is now found in many French churches and cathedrals; a particularly fine example is the one in the church of St Symphorien at Azay-le-Rideau. One of the most distinctive and feminine is the white marble statue in her own village of Domrémy-la-Pucelle. Some occultists view her mission in France as being of great importance to the future history of Europe, and several books have been written about her supposed secret missions, some based on the theory that she was working for an esoteric school within the Catholic Church.

Joan's story begins in Chinon and ends in Rouen. Before she met the Dauphin, she had waited for two days in an inn below the castle of Chinon, and the story of how the King hid among the crowd of 300 aristocrats, and yet was so easily identified by the humble god-directed Maid, has become the very stuff of legend. Even so, her death at Rouen is even more beset with legend than the beginning of the story at Chinon, for there are some who insist that it was not Joan who was burned but a volunteer substitute. There are some records which suggest that Joan was present at later battles against the English, yet, while it is clear that the documents relating to her trial and death are not genuine, there seems little doubt that she did not escape the pyre. Had she done so, then the whole of France would have known, and indeed the course of French and English history would have been very different.

Statue of Joan of Arc, in the parish church at Azay-le-Rideau. If the number of the statues in France is anything to go by, there may be no doubt that Joan is by far the most popular saint in that country.

GILLES DE RAIS EXECUTED AT NANTES

The case of Gilles de Rais is as overtly political as Joan's, just as corrupt, and yet, in popular literature at least, he has never been rehabilitated, and his name still represents (quite wrongly) the darkest form of witchcraft. Gilles de Laval, the Baron of Rais, was one of the richest nobles in France, and after his marriage to the heiress Catherine of Thouars, his wealth was increased tenfold. He had many estates and châteaux scattered throughout France; some of them, including those at Tiffauges and Champtocé-sur-Loire, (now standing in desolate yet romantic ruin) are famous as 'Bluebeard' castles, and remain associated by local people with witchcraft legends.

For all his wealth, Gilles was profligate and eventually he turned to the art of alchemy in order to learn the secret of making gold from base metal. After his initial failures, he met the famous Florentine necromancer, Francesco Prelati, who took lodgings near the parish church of St Nicolas, in nearby St-Florent-la-Vieil, when he became the official demonologist of the Baron, then living in the magnificent château of Tiffauges. Even before Gilles had elected to occupy Tiffauges, it had gained a sinister reputation, for legend said that it was built by Melusine, a snake-woman who was the offspring of an amorous laison between King Elinas of Albania and a fairy.

So far as we may determine from the records, Prelati was an alchemist who depended upon the operations of demons rather than upon the use of alchemical instruments and research to achieve his ends. He organised what have since been called 'seances' for the baron. These were not seances in the modern sense of the word, but the direct invocation of particular demons who, according to the grimoire literature of the time, were supposed to have full knowledge of alchemical transmutation which they were prepared (for a price, of course) to make available to magicians. In the later trials it was claimed that Prelati eventually turned to the 'full rituals' in such conjuration: these,

The ruins of the once-magnificent castle at Champtocé-sur-Loire, formerly owned by Gilles de Rais.

The signature of Gilles de Rais, from a document recording the sale of one of his many castles to the Duke of Brittany, in 1439.

Opposite: the castle at Chinon, from across the Loire, where Joan recognised the Dauphin, who had been hidden among his courtiers to fool the Maid.

as outlined in the more gory grimoires, demanded the blood of sacrificed children. However, in the list of his personal effects, recorded during the trials, it is clear that he dealt merely with standard invocations, for he carried only a ritual sword and a magical stone, the *dyadocus*, used for divination. Despite this, the sensationalist literature concerning Gilles often includes accounts of the large number of local children who 'mysteriously' disappeared from the countryside near his châteaux. Interestingly enough, these accounts were not substantiated in the later trials, even though a whole barrage of innuendo in the form of unsubstantiated witness and hearsay was sworn.

In 1440 Geoffroi le Ferron purchased one of Gilles' castles at St Étienne de Malemort. Due to a piece of foolishness or a misunderstanding, the Baron offended le Ferron's brother, who was a priest. The local Bishop used this as an excuse to level charges against Gilles. Without question, the main purpose underlying this action was greed, for the Bishop and the Inquisition knew that if the charges were sustained, they would acquire all the Baron's wealth and extensive properties.

A view of one of the medieval buildings in St Florent-la-Vieil, where the famous Florentine alchemist and necromancer, Francesco Prelati, lodged during the months he worked as the official demonologist and alchemist for Gilles de Rais in the fifteenth century.

Almost all the accusations levelled against Gilles were a tissue of lies based on hearsay and imagination, yet they presented the Baron in a most hideous light, as the following short passage from the long indictment indicates:

> The aforesaid Gilles de Rais, accused, (and his accomplices) have taken innocent boys and girls, and inhumanly butchered, killed, dismembered, burned and otherwise tortured them, and the said Gilles, accused, has immolated the bodies of the said innocents to devils, invoked and sacrificed to evil spirits, and has foully committed the sin of sodomy with young boys and in other ways lusted against nature after young girls, spurning the natural way of copulation, while both the innocent boys and girls were alive or sometimes dead or even sometimes in their death throes.

It was further claimed that the bodies of these child victims were thrown into ditches and cesspools of the castles at La Suze and Tiffauges.

Although at first he denied all such charges, Gilles was put to torture, as were a number of his alleged accomplices – though, significantly, none of his own 500 servants were called in evidence. Under terrible torture one of his associates confessed to seeing Gilles debauch young children. Another, Étienne Corillaut, told the court that he had personally counted the decapitated bodies of at least 36 children in the castle, and had heard Gilles confess his enjoyment at having sexual union with children while they were dying in agony. Gilles finally confessed to these acts, even elaborating upon them to the point of ridicule. Evidence obtained under torture was admissable in French law at that time, and he was accordingly found guilty by all the three courts that tried him. The Inquisition found him condemned of apostasy, heresy and invocation (of demons); the Bishop found him guilty of sodomy, sacrilege and the violation of ecclesiastical privileges, while the Civil Court, which alone could issue a death sentence, confirmed that he was guilty of murder. He was condemend to death on that charge – though it is often recorded that he was condemned and executed as a witch.

At Nantes, on 26 October 1440, Gilles was hanged, and his body placed on a funeral pyre in a ceremonial gesture. His relatives were given permission to remove the body before it was burned and to bury it in the local Carmelite church. His vast properties and riches were awarded to his accusers and judges.

CHARLES LELAND AND THE WICCAN TRADITION

Modern witchcraft is to some extent a watered-down affair in comparison with the bizarre world of the medieval witchscare legends. Undoubtedly though, sabbats involving sexual practices are still held by groups of people who believe that the lower nature, linked with the great god Pan, should be served by some form of ritual. It is a strange fact that the spread of modern witchcraft in Europe owed a great deal to an American: the remarkable Charles Leland. He was born in Philadelphia in 1824 and was a veteran of both the European revolution of 1848 and the American Civil War (even seeing action at Gettysburg). Eventually he settled in Florence, where he befriended a young woman named Maddalena, who confided in him that she was a witch. Intrigued by her stories, Leland joined her coven and collected many of its traditional rituals, which he published in London, in 1899, under the title *Aradia: the Gospel of the Witches*. Leland took from the Florentine coven those elements which he imagined to represent the genuine rituals, and used them as the basis for his own revival of pagan witchcraft, the wiccan.

The importance of *Aradia* lies mainly in its influence on Gerald Gardner, who was involved with the English Ordo Templi Orientalis (see page 25), supposedly based on ancient Templar rituals. Gardner, a friend of Aleister Crowley, eventually settled in Castletown on the Isle of Man. The house had already been converted by a previous owner into a museum of historical witchcraft, and Gardner improved upon it considerably. Eventually the entire collection passed to the United States.

While the majority of witches who follow Leland's wiccan tradition tend to practise in secret, a number of private notebooks or grimoires belonging to recent covens are lodged in private and public collections, for example the manuscript

Page from a personal grimoire, produced in the fifties of this century by one of the followers of the Crowley magical cult.

(illustrated on this page) which was written and illustrated by a follower of the Crowley tradition of magic. At the beginning of this notebook is a curious map of a part of Yorkshire, which marks out six sites of special occult or magical significance in an area which is termed The Land of the Dragon, each site being given an appropriate symbol. The castle at Skipton is represented, and so are Bolton Abbey, the prehistoric Swastika Stone at Ilkley and the supposed Templar monument in the town of Keighley. Crude symbols represent a burning fire at Baildon, probably because it was supposed that this village was once the centre of the worship of the ancient fire god Baal, from which it was believed the name for the village was derived. Equally crude is the drawing of a magic book, presumably the grimoire itself, which represents Bingley, where the writer of the book lived. The purpose behind this fascinating map is probably to locate by means of the central inverted triangle with its triple radiant the place where all these magical elements meet – namely, the place of the Sabbat, or the place where the magicial rites should be practised. The interesting thing is that this focal point is on Baildon Moor, which for centuries has been reputed to be a meeting place for witches.

ALEISTER CROWLEY, BLACK MAGIC IN ENGLAND AND SICILY

One modern magician was undoubtedly influenced by the popular stories of Gilles de Rais. This is Aleister Crowley, the self-styled Great Beast, who is perhaps more infamous than he deserves to be, even though he certainly practised black magic. He succeeded in creating an image of himself as a powerful magician, but with a persona which savours more of a selfish and spoilt child than anything distinctly magical. The place in Europe most intimately linked with Crowley is the farmhouse on the hill above Cefalu in Sicily, which he rented in 1920, and called somewhat grandly the Abbey of Thelema. The name was taken from Theleme, the country where the monk in Rabelais's *Gargantua and Pantagruel* built a fantastic abbey. In Greek *thelema* means will, and so in the choice of the name Crowley was making a play on his own adage 'Do what thou wilt, is the whole of the Law' – undoubtedly a recipe for unbridled egotism. It was at the farmhouse that Crowley gave himself over to black magic rites, the taking of a wide range of hallucinogenic drugs, painting very bad pictures, and indulging in sexual orgies with his two mistressses and a variety of friends.

The signature used by Aleister Crowley in his autohagiography, *The Confessions*, is of considerable interest owing to the phallic capital A, which offended so many people that Crowley found it difficult to sell the book when it was first published. However, while undoubtedly phallic, the symbol A is also linked with the sigil used by astrologers to denote the ascending node of the Moon, the so-called Dragon's Head ☊ . This suggests that Crowley intended the A to have at least two meanings, for it could easily be associated with Crowley's *nom de plume*, the Great Beast. For all his popular fame as a powerful magician, towards the end of his life Crowley was little more than an egotistical drug-addict, living in a small boarding house near Hastings, and injecting himself daily with ten times the normally lethal dose of heroin, merely for survival.

When the director Kenneth Angers made his film at the farmhouse in Cefalu, a few of the grotesque paintings were still on the walls, a reminder that Crowley had lined his ritual sanctum with lewd images which looked down upon a red-tiled floor painted with a pentagram inscribed in the manner set out in the popular grimoires. Although many of the things which Crowley claimed seem, on examination, to have been fictitious, it is recorded that during his time in Sicily he did actually perform blood sacrifices involving animals and birds. Terrible as this undoubtedly was, we may be relieved that he did not take matters quite so far as a later boast implied, which was that he had sacrificed male children 'of perfect innocence and high intelligence' at least three times each week over a span of fifteen years. If there was any purpose at all in such an absurd, drug-ridden boast, it was merely to claim his superiority over the Frenchman Gilles de Rais, whose story he had so completely misunderstood.

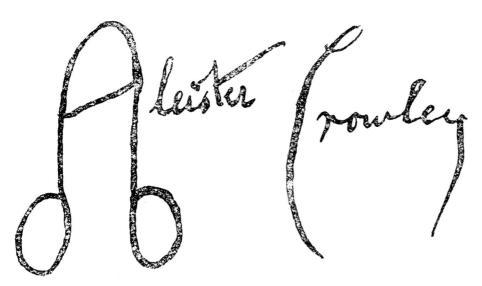

The signature of Aleister Crowley, with the distinctive phallic capital letter A.

3 Planets, Zodiacs and Stars

THE island of Hveen (now Ven), in the Sound near Elsinor, is one of the most intriguing places of all for those interested in astrology. In the sixteenth century the island was given in trust by King Frederick II of Denmark to the astronomer-astrologer Tycho Brahe, who planned to spend his life in the study of the stars and planets, and who wanted a place where he could build his own observatory. Before making his way to Hveen, Brahe fulfilled one request made by the king – that he should give a series of lectures on the art of astrology at the University of Copenhagen, for while it was astronomy which fascinated Brahe, it was astrology which intrigued the king and most of his subjects. In those days the occult arts were openly taught in universities, and an interest in astrology was widespread throughout Scandinavia.

Brahe was born in Knudstrup in Scania, then in Denmark but now part of Sweden, the son of a Danish nobleman who was also an astronomer. His horoscope for 14 December 1546 has been preserved, and from this it is possible to see the extent to which Brahe used his own chart to determine his actions throughout life. For example, the year 1574, when Frederick made the gift of Hveen to Tycho, was of great importance in the horoscope. Brahe was 28 years old – a year which, as a proficient astrologer, he would have recognised as being a key date in his personal chart. He would have been aware that since his own planet Mars was in the sign of Aries, his most important research would be conducted in a place ruled by that sign. From his familiarity with the occult tradition he would also have known that in the astrological tradition, his beloved Denmark was ruled by Aries; this would have led him to realise that if he were to achieve his life's work it would be important for him to stay within the influence of Aries. We may be sure, therefore, that Tycho would have examined his natal chart with real pleasure when the king made his offer, and would have accepted the proposal with great joy, aware that it was a call of destiny.

Overleaf: a view of Florence at sunset, from the Piazzale Michelangelo.

Tycho Brahe's observatory on the island of Hveen was one of the last to be built in Europe on the lines of the huge stellar observatories built in Islamic countries in preceding centuries. This woodcut and the one opposite are from *Tychonis Brahe Dani Episolarum Astronomicarum Libri*, published in Frankfurt in 1610.

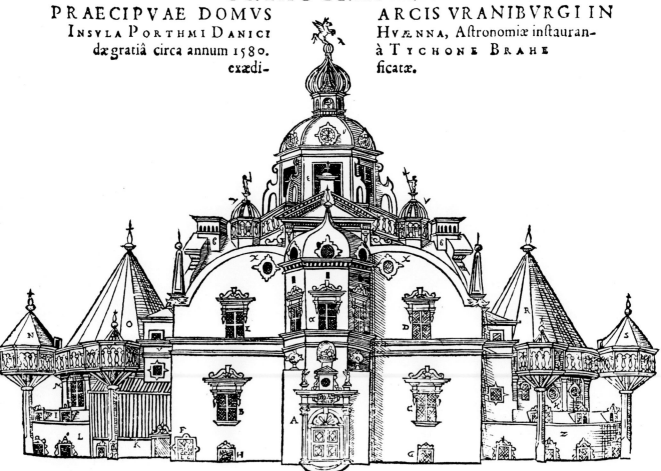

ORTHOGRAPHIA

PRAECIPVAE DOMVS
INSVLA PORTHMI DANICI
dæ gratiâ circa annum 1580.
cxædi-

ARCIS VRANIBVRGI IN
HVÆNNA, Aſtronomiæ inſtauran-
à TYCHONE BRAHE
ficatæ.

Brahe had studied law at the University of Copenhagen (where in 1560 he observed an eclipse of the Sun, which gave him an interest in astronomy and astrology) and then at Leipzig, universities which were among the most advanced in their day in the study of stellar lore and mathematics. From 1558 onwards, he made some astrological predictions in which he related the effects of certain eclipses to events connected with the ruling house of Denmark and Norway. It was apparently this study which brought him to the attention of the remarkable Frederick II, and led the king to encourage his work.

On 30 August 1576, according to astrological principles, Tycho laid the foundations for his new stellar observatory at Uraniborg. He noted that the Sun was rising over the horizon in Leo, along with the expansive and beneficial Jupiter near the powerful star Regulus, and the Moon setting in the opposite sign of Aquarius. Naturally, these factors governing the choice of a good moment to begin such an important enterprise were also linked with Tycho's own personal chart, for his ascendant was in Aquarius, along with the planets Venus and Jupiter, and his descendant in Aquarius. This 'castle of the stars' was actually a house and observatory built according to designs drawn up by Brahe himself.

Within the main building of the castle he constructed a number of remarkable instruments. In his subterranean observatory, which was decorated with huge frescoes depicting eight great astronomers, there was a huge mural quadrant by which he could determine with greater accuracy than ever before the altitudes of the celestial bodies. Soon Uraniborg became a centre for stellar research and the teaching of astrology, and students flocked from all parts of Europe in search of instruction and knowledge.

In 1577, Frederick II's son and heir, the future Christian IV, was born. According to the custom of the day, a horoscope was required for the child, and Tycho was called

Another view of Tycho Brahe's observatory. Although his original instruments are no longer at Hveen, drawings and plans show they had striking resemblance to those still *in situ* in the great Islamic observatories in India, such as those at Jaipur and Delhi.

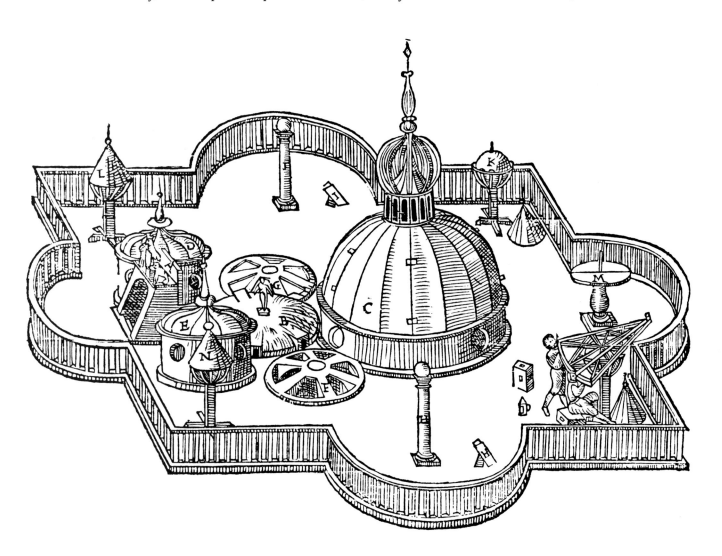

from Uraniborg to Copenhagen to cast it. This horoscope is still preserved, along with the astrological and meteorological diary Tycho kept with his assistant Elias Olsen. In the birth chart for Christian IV, one of several very complex astrological charts which he drew up for the members of the Danish royal family, Tycho became one of the first astrologers to use the system of calculations proposed by Copernicus, rather than depending on the less accurate tables of Ptolemaic system used by other astrologers, and called the Alfonsine tables.

During his time at Hveen, Brahe made a detailed study of the nova (a new or exploding star), which had appeared in the constellation of Cassiopeia in 1572. Assuming that such an extraordinary phenomenon would be sure to influence the human world, he made some somewhat gloomy predictions. He also demonstrated that the comets were in motion above the Moon, not below it. These proofs were to have a most profound influence on scientific thinking, for until that time it had been believed that changes, such as the erratic movement of the comets or the birth of a new star, could not take place in the realms beyond the lunar sphere.

The exploding stars which we now call novas had deep implications for Brahe, for he saw that they disproved the theological theory that God had created the world in a single, complete and final act. This 'star' of 1572 could not be explained in terms of anything which was then known, and its appearance (and its subsequent disappearance) caused much consternation in astrological and astronomical circles. Indeed, it has often been said by historians that the new star of 1572 had a greater effect on the learned world than the publication of Copernicus's revolutionary theory in 1543. The new star did indeed have a most extraordinary influence on the thinking of Tycho's day, for until then men had accepted Aristotle's thesis that the spheres beyond that of the Moon were immutable and, unlike our familiar world, were not subject to change and decay. There had always been a distinction drawn between the changeable nature of the earth, and all earthly things, and what was thought to be the changeless, serene realm of the celestial. Tycho showed that the comets and novas, among the most changeable and erratic phenomena in the skies, were indeed part of that celestial realm. This notion, born in the curious castle of instruments, changed Man's view of the universe even more profoundly than the Copernican dictum that the Sun was the centre of our solar system.

Apparently as a result of studying the effects of the impressive comet of 1577 which, as a practising astrologer, he saw as a portent of future events, and by studying the tables of planetary positions for the future, Tycho was able to predict that in 1592 a male child would be born in northern Europe who would have an important destiny: 'In the North, in Finland', he wrote, 'there will be born a Prince who will lay waste Germany, and vanish in 1632.' He further pronounced that this man would die in 1632 'in a religious battle'. In 1594 Gustavus Adolphus, the future King of Sweden was born. He was to become the most able statesman and general of his time, successfully resisting the expansionist aspirations of the Austrian general Wallenstein, and compelling a redefinition of the Swedish borders with Russia and Poland. Napoleon was later to describe Gustavus Adolphus as the supreme military genius of the seventeenth century, and he was without doubt the greatest ruler that Sweden has ever had. After a lifetime of service to his country, he died in action, as Tycho has predicted, at the battle of Lutzen in 1632, but not before realising that the battle had been won by his own Swedish troops.

It is perhaps curious that a man who had such undoubted ability as an astrologer should have found the art somewhat distasteful. In a letter dated 1587 Tycho wrote 'Each year I provide an astrological forecast for my master the King, whose wishes I must comply with, though personally I regard such matters as trivial and dislike such dubious prophecies. This is not the way to the truth. The true way is found in geometry and arithmetic; these, together with a studious observation of the heavens, are the basis of astronomy.' For all his outstanding genius, Tycho was in this respect a child of his time, for astrology, the passion of learned men for almost 2,000 years, was rapidly giving way to astronomy. This was not because astrology itself was regarded as an invalid art, but because the new scientific outlook had little interest in its rules, and predictive techniques, which were associated – albeit wrongly – with the black arts. It was these which they found distasteful or foreign to their own interests.

Tycho worked at Uraniborg for over 20 years, until the death of Frederick II in 1588. The successor to the throne was not interested in astrology, and Tycho, lacking royal protection, was exposed to the criticism of his noble peers who failed to understand his work. When the funding for Uraniborg was withdrawn, he was compelled to abandon the castle for good.

JOHANNES KEPLER

After leaving Hveen, Tycho went to live under the protection of the Holy Roman Emperor, Rudolph II, who was fascinated by all occult studies and, recognising Tycho's worth, established him in an observatory at Benatek, near Prague. It was there, almost in the last year of his life, that Tycho met the young Johannes Kepler, already a proficient astrologer. Kepler gladly became the assistant of the Danish astronomer, from whom he learned a great deal about the occult arts – especially astrology and alchemy. Tycho made available to Kepler all the results of his immense stellar and solar research from Uraniborg: this later enabled Kepler to formulate his three famous laws of planetary motion. Thus it can be claimed that the most important scientific discovery of the seventeenth century was initiated in the strange castle of Uraniborg.

Kepler is not usually thought of as an astrologer because his astronomical and mathematical discoveries have tended to overshadow his interest in occult matters. However, surviving documents show that Kepler, like his mentor, and Sir Isaac Newton who was interested in alchemy, was fascinated by many things which we would now consider occult. He is also known to have cast many thousands of horoscopes in an attempt to explore the validity of that ancient science.

He cast several horoscopes for the remarkable Austrian general and statesman Albert von Wallenstein, who was a great enthusiast for astrology and alchemy; from his calculations Kepler attempted to determine the outcome of the war Wallenstein was fighting against Denmark. The general did not rely only on Kepler for the art of prediction, however: records indicate that he had the horoscope of Gustavus Adolphus cast by another astrologer, a Doctor Herlicius, in order to try and find out what the outcome of the war would be.

How accurate were Kepler's astrological predictions? It is recorded that he correctly foretold that Wallenstein would be defeated by the Danish, and later by Gustavus Adolphus of Sweden; he also appears to have given some indication of his defeat by the Swedish troops at the battle of Lutzen. Kepler had to exercise considerable discretion in the way in which he formulated his predictions for Wallenstein, for the general had also learned how to interpret charts. He had to be particularly careful when it came to the matter of calculating from the chart the time of the general's death, and he solved this problem by pointing out that from certain important oppositions in the general's chart the years from 1632 to 1634 would herald very great difficulties which would reach a crisis in 1634. Wallenstein was assassinated on 25 February 1634. The fact that Kepler did not say in so many words that the assassination would take place at that time has been misinterpreted by later historians, who maintain that Kepler got the chart wrong. However, one must not forget that a good astrologer is always reluctant to tell a person when death might be expected because of the psychological effect that this has on the subject's life. Some things are best not known.

THE ZODIAC IN ART AND ARCHITECTURE

Uraniborg at Hveen is probably the most remarkable survival of the practical interest which combined astrology with astronomy. However, in a less practical sense – that is, in relation to art and symbolism – Europe is full of survivals from the age when astrology was regarded as the Queen of Sciences: in different parts of Europe there are still very many important buildings dedicated to cosmological lore. We shall note one or two of these architectural wonders, which incorporate zodiacal imagery in their decoration and so on, in the context of cosmic orientation on in chapter 4. However, the most important centres in Europe are those which involve cycles of paintings dedicated to the more serious aspects of astrology – to zodiacal, planetary or constellational

One of the 666 esoteric frescoes
from the Salone in Padua. The
image shows zodiacal Gemini, but
the imagery also relates to the
constellation Gemini, the history of
which is linked with the story of
Castor and Pollux, one of whom
was immortal, the other mortal.

imagery. Among these cycles, perhaps the most impressive is that in the Salone in
Padua, which contains, among the 666 remarkable esoteric frescoes, the twelve images
of the zodiac, the seven planets, and a series of pictures connected with an almost-
defunct astrological tradition relating to the 36 decanates, derived from a division of
each of the twelve signs of the zodiac into three equal parts.

The decanate system was popular among esoteric artists in the early Renaissance,
and it is for this reason that we find a whole room in the Palazzo di Schifanoia in Ferrara
dedicated to what are now called the Months, but which were originally known as the
Decanates. As we can see from one of the surviving frescoes all the signs of the zodiac
are linked with three images, each of which represents the tradition (derived by way of
Arabic lore) relating to the relevant decane, or ten-degree division of the 30-degree sign.
Most zodiacal and constellational frescoes are less complex than these, though some of
them are on a larger scale. The constellational series which decorates the enormous

The three decans of zodiacal Aries in the Palazzo di Schifanoia, Ferrara. Aries itself is the ram, leaping over the Sun, while the three decan images are represented by three people, two men and one woman. The curious imagery and symbolism attached to these decans is derived from Arabian astrological lore.

Below: detail of the central ceiling panel of the Constellations fresco cycle in the Chiericati Palace, Vicenza. Luna (the Moon) with her traditional crescent at her head, is driving two white horses.

ceiling of the Chiericati Palace in Vicenza incorporates images relating to the zodiac, most of which are related to Greek and Roman coinage designs, as well as to the famous prints of the constellations produced by the German artist Durer in 1515, according to the descriptions of Heinfogel and Stabius. The other comparable Italian astrological ceiling is in the Chigi Palace, Rome.

Far more common than astrological frescos, and usually much earlier in date, are the large number of zodiacal and planetary programmes found in marble and stone on the façades of medieval churches and cathedrals. The most remarkable sculpted series are found in Italy and France, the oldest cycle being in the gaunt monastery of the Sacra di San Michele, in the Val di Susa; and in such cities as Florence – in the medieval baptistry and in the church of San Miniato al Monte, inside the octagonal baptistry at Parma, Amiens cathedral, Chartres cathedral, the abbey-church of La Madeleine at Vézelay, in the Notre-Dame-des-Miracles at Mauriac, and in Ste-Croix at Bordeaux.

Although the finest of the zodiacs are Italian and French, astrological imagery is found widely throughout Europe: for example, there is a beautifully-preserved fifteenth-century series on the underarch of the Fitzjames Arch at Merton College in Oxford. The largest medieval example in England is that in the marble floor of the Trinity Chapel at Canterbury Cathedral.

One of the many zodiacal images in the city of Florence. These four symbols are part of a complete series on the fountain in the square opposite the medieval Signoria.

One of the zodiacal stele by the thirteenth-century sculptor Antelami, now in the baptistry at Parma. This stele portrays the zodiacal image of Sagittarius as an unmounted bowman, and the corresponding labour of the month.

Part of the zodiacal band in the porch of Ste-Croix, in Bordeaux. Above the central figure is the female figure of Libra, holding the scales, and at the figure's feet with its back to us is the curious form of Scorpio.

Details of the zodiacal images on the northern portico of the west front at Chartres cathedral. The images of the zodiac alternate with the labours of the months. The inner archvolt shows, in the lower register, the ram of Aries: in the higher register is the horned bull of Taurus. In the outer archbolt, lower register, is the crab of Cancer, and in the upper register the lion of Leo. Gemini is missing. This is part of the esoteric plan at Chartres, for Gemini is shown on another doorway in the guise of the Templar twins, pointing down to the ever-important fish of Christ-Pisces (see page 24).

INTERPRETING ZODIACAL SYMBOLISM

The complexity of the astrological designs in cathedrals and churches are a reminder of the importance of astrology in the early medieval period, when the stellar lore of the Greek and Roman past, which had been preserved by the Arabs, was being reintroduced into Europe. The symbols and images of zodiacs and planets, and their relevance to the Christian message are often well-hidden in such programmes, and are frequently misunderstood by historians. Thus the only satisfactory way to study them is to visit the churches and see them for oneself, and to attempt to work out their true significance by means of observation and thought. As a guide to such a personal approach, however, we may take the zodiacal roundels on the upper half-circle of the tympanum in the narthex of the Madeleine at Vézelay. These are part of the huge sculptural programme completed in the first half of the twelfth century.

The theme of the tympanum deals with the mission following upon Pentecost and, consequently, most of the symbolic details are linked with the notion of the spread of the Gospel into the different parts of the earth. The symbolic function of these zodiacal roundels is to indicate that the mission of Christ is of a cosmic nature: the events of history depicted below are, therefore, to be viewed as being in accord with the dictates of the Heavens as expressed through the stars.

If we examine the roundels closely, we see that not all of those depicting the zodiac correspond to the standard forms with which we are now familiar – this is probably because these images were derived from Arabic sources which have since been lost. For example, the image for the twins of Gemini is represented here unconventionally as a

The inner doorway of the narthex at Vézelay. In the outer semi-circle of the tympanum are the images of the twelve signs of the zodiac in stylistic forms which leave no doubt that they were derived from Islamic zodiacal manuscripts. Details are shown overleaf.

Two zodiacal roundels from the narthex tympanum of Vézelay. In the bottom circle is Sagittarius as a mounted horseman, shooting at the Scorpion which precedes him, while in the central roundel there is a camel-like creature which represents Scorpio, with an enormous poisonous tail.

single figure with two heads and two pairs of arms. Scorpio, the sixth roundel along the arch, on the left of Christ, looks much like an eight-legged camel; while Taurus, the eighth along the arch to the right of Christ, has the tail of a fish.

The twelve signs are all located within the series of roundels, starting with Aquarius to the bottom right of Christ, and continuing round to the goat-fish Capricorn, on the left. The other roundels represent the months – for example, the first depicts January, symbolized by a peasant cutting bread, while the last in the series represents December, symbolized by a man with wine. Because of its connection with the Eucharist, this important liquid obviously points to the hidden significance of the 'blood of Christ', quite relevant to the month in which we now believe Jesus was born. It is worth noting that this last roundel *completes* the arch which began with the image of a peasant cutting bread – thus, the two Christian 'mysteries' of Bread and Wine play an important role in the symbolism of the tympanum, and we must presume that one of the tacit implications is that the Apostles are to spread the good news of these two Mysteries of Christ. One may see from this analysis, which is by no means exhaustive, that it is not possible to understand the deeper symbolism of such medieval schemes without reference to astrological lore.

Most of the vast medieval zodiacal cycles are linked with esoteric programmes involving the use of certain symbols for secret purposes. This means that it is difficult to deal with the deeper aspects of specific programmes in brief: however, further notes on zodiacal symbolism in relation to orientation are contained in the chapter 4 and these lead to the deeper implications of the major European zodiacal cycles.

ZODIACAL CLOCKS

In the face of this complex medieval and Renaissance astrological lore, it is almost a relief to turn to the relatively simple 'zodiacal clocks' which are found in various parts of Europe. The symbolism underlying most zodical clocks is intended to suggest that human activity, regulated by time itself, is also regulated by cosmic realities. In some cases, for example in the splendid fifteenth-century clock in Berne, the zodiac is incorporated into the actual clock mechanism. In other cases, however, such as the modern example at Worms, zodiac and clock are represented separately. The design of the zodiacal clock at Haguenau, in Germany, combines stellar imagery with a month-indicator as well as the diurnal clock, the whole face being so complicated that it is difficult to actually tell the time from it.

One of the most lovely series of modern zodiacal roundels, from the zodiacal clock on the façade of the Town Hall at Worms.

Berne is a city with many buildings and statues of occult significance, of which the fifteenth-century clocktower is one. A close-up view of the zodiacal clock is shown below.

The zodiacal and planetary imagery on the medieval clock in Berne offers an interesting example of how early clocks were as much used for zodiacal time-keeping as with recording the passing of the hours. Although complex in its mechanism, this Berne clock is relatively simple in comparison with the model inside the cathedral at Strasbourg, which is perhaps the most sophisticated of all zodiacal mechanical clocks.

The most extensive series of zodiacal clocks is in Italy, and fine examples – most of them of relatively early date – are found in Venice, Modena, Padua and Cremona, all of which have been restored in relatively recent times. In England the two finest examples are the eighteenth-century sundial in the first court of Queen's College in Cambridge, and the clockface over the main entrance to the offices of the *Financial Times* in Cannon Street, in the City of London. The latter was designed in 1959 by the engineering firm of Thwaites and Reed, and is probably the finest modern example in the world.

Painted sundials often incorporate zodiacal and planetary imagery. In Germany there are several fine examples of which the most noteworthy is that on the Ratskeller façade at Würzburg; it is thoroughly modern in that it incorporates sigils for the most recently discovered planets: Uranus, Pluto and Neptune. The planets are merely schematic, and play no part in recording time, as the presence of the sigil for the Earth itself indicates. The 'occult village' of Rennes-le-Château, in southern France, displays two sigil-bearing sundials, one on an ancient look-out tower and the other incised into the stonework above a door.

The face of the zodiacal clock in St Mark's Square, Venice, with the gilt zodiacal images in relief. The hand which marks out the progression through the zodiacal signs is marked with the image of a solar head.

The modern zodiacal clock at Bracken House, in London, designed by Thwaites and Reed in 1959, is certainly the most impressive zodiac in London – perhaps, indeed, the finest modern example of zodiacal clockmaking in the world.

Below: a fine example of a medieval zodiacal sundial, on the façade of the old Ratshaus, in Würzburg. The presence of the sigils for the three modern planets – Uranus, Neptune and Pluto – indicate that the sundial has been restored in relatively modern times.

Constellation charts are often confused with zodiacal charts because in the constellations there are twelve images with similar names to those used to denote the twelve signs of the zodiac. However, the constellations relating to these twelve names are not of equal size – for example, the constellation of Aries is extremely small, while that of Leo is enormous. In contrast, the twelve signs of the zodiac are of equal length, consisting of 30 degree arcs. This chart of the northern hemisphere of constellations is by Phillip Lea, 1686.

Another strain of zodiacal and constellational symbolism is found in statuary which evokes the notion of the cosmos, in the manner of the old pictorial star-charts. A very fine example is that in the gardens in front of the Palace of Nations, in Geneva. It is clearly intended to suggest that the United Nations have the same spiritual harmony as the union of constellational images, which find their rightful places in the skies.

The occult tradition has always insisted that there is a relationship between parts of the world and parts of the stellar realm, and the interesting thing is that certain of the ancient occult traditions regarding the influences of the stars may still be found in Europe. In some cases, for example at Rennes-le-Château, Paris, Glastonbury and in northern France, the traditional zodiacal influences attributed to a locality or area have been linked with complex zodiacal patterns and star-maps; these can (it is claimed) be traced on the earth itself. A large-scale orientation pattern linked with the zodiacal sign Virgo is traced on the map of northern France, relating certain towns and cities by means of their churches dedicated to the Virgin Mary. This 'Virgoan' orientation pattern is typical of other patterns which occultists have traced over parts of Europe.

The possibility of so tracing patterns arises essentially out of the idea that each part of the world, and each city or town, falls under the rule of a single zodiacal sign or planet. There are many lists of what are officially called chorographies, but the most widely used is the one based on the writings of Ptolemy, the second-century astrologer whose books were very influential in the medieval period. The main rulers for European countries given in such lists are as follows.

England, France and Germany are under Aries. Ireland is under Taurus, Scotland is under Cancer and Wales is under Gemini – though some astrologers link this country with Capricorn. Italy is under the rule of Leo, Spain under Sagittarius, but, as we shall see, some astrologers claim that this country is ruled by Taurus. Holland is one of the countries ruled by Cancer, perhaps because its life is so intimately involved with water,

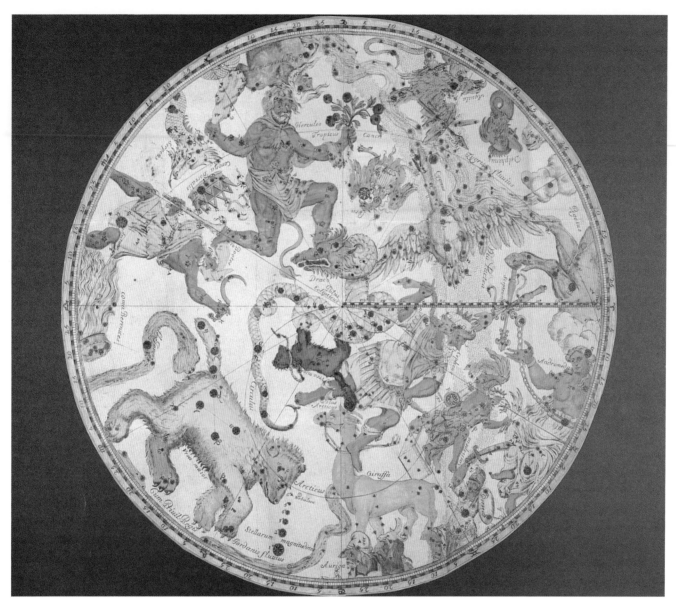

Above: an Arabian star map, reproduced in a coloured lithograph of the nineteenth century. To the top right of the circle is the Great Bear. A large number of the star names used in Europe are corruptions of Arabian star names.

A huge constellational globe stands in the gardens of the Palace of Nations in Geneva. The symbolism suggests that the harmony of the star patterns might one day be mirrored on each.

Zodiacal rulerships in western Europe

Key to Sigils

The following alphabetical lists show the traditional zodiacal rulerships, a few of which are disputed by some modern astrologers. Only the places mentioned in the main body of the text are included.

CITY

RULERSHIPS

ARIES
Cracow
Faenza
Florence
Leicester
Marseilles
Naples
Padua
Saragossa
Utrecht

TAURUS
Bologna
Dublin
Leipzig
Mantua
Palermo
Parma

GEMINI
Cordova
London
Louvain
Nuremberg

CANCER
Amsterdam
Berne
Cadiz
Lübeck
Milan
Venice
Vicenza
York

LEO
Bath
Bristol
Delphi
Prague
Portsmouth
Ravenna
Rome

VIRGO
Basle
Cheltenham
Ferrara
Heidelberg
Lyon
Paris
Reading

LIBRA
Antwerp
Frankfurt
Lisbon
Siena
Vienna

SCORPIO
Cremona
Ghent
Liverpool
Piacenza

SAGITTARIUS
Avignon
Cologne
Naples
Narbonne

CAPRICORN
Modena

AQUARIUS
Bremen
Brighton
Hamburg

PISCES
Ratisbon
Santiago
  de Compostela
Seville
Worms

COUNTRY

RULERSHIPS

ARIES
England
France
Germany

TAURUS
Ireland
(Eire and Northern Ireland)
Spain
(Spain is also ascribed to
Sagittarius by some
astrologers)

GEMINI
Wales

CANCER
Holland
Scotland

LEO
Italy

VIRGO
Switzerland

CAPRICORN
Greece

POLAND

CZECHOSLOVAKIA

Cracow

Vienna

HUNGARY

RUMANIA

YUGOSLAVIA

BULGARIA

ALBANIA

GREECE

TURKEY

ITALY

Naples

Delphi

Key		
Zodiacal sign	Image	Sigil
Aries	Ram	♈
Taurus	Bull	♉
Gemini	Twins	♊
Cancer	Crab (Crayfish)	♋
Leo	Lion	♌
Virgo	Woman	♍
Libra	Scales	♎
Scorpio	Scorpion	♏
Sagittarius	Horseman archer	♐
Capricorn	Goat-fish	♑
Aquarius	Waterman	♒
Pisces	Fishes	♓

Detail of the Marines' Memorial in Portsmouth. The compass point set in the marble surface is a radiant star, reminding us that the city is traditionally ruled by Leo and therefore by our nearest star, the Sun of our solar system.

Below: there are numerous parks and lakes in Seville, a city which is traditionally ruled by watery Pisces.

Some astrologers say that Paris is ruled by Leo, and to support their argument they point to the ground plan of the modern city, which is based on a radiant star, L'Étoile. However, traditionally the city is ruled by Virgo, which is not surprising because Paris, and several surrounding towns and cities, echo on earth the stellar plan of the constellation Virgo.

and depends so completely upon the sea. Another good example of a 'watery' place being ruled by Cancer is that of Venice, with its teeming canal life and a now-fading glory built upon the sea-trade.

Among other important cities, Florence, Leicester, Marseilles and Padua are ruled by Aries. Bologna, Dublin, Palermo and Parma are ruled by Taurus. Cordova, London and Louvain are ruled by Gemini. Amsterdam, Berne, Cadiz, Lübeck, Milan and Venice are ruled by Cancer. Bristol, Portsmouth, Ravenna and Rome are ruled by Leo. Basle, Ferrara, Heidelberg, Lyon and Paris are ruled by Virgo. Antwerp, Frankfurt, Siena and Vienna are ruled by Libra. Cremona, Ghent, Liverpool and Piacenza are ruled by Scorpio. Avignon, Cologne, Naples and Narbonne are ruled by Sagittarius. Bremen, Brighton and Hamburg are ruled by Aquarius. Santiago de Compostella, Ratisbon, Seville and Worms are ruled by Pisces.

Above: the city of Florence is ruled by zodiacal Aries, while Italy is ruled by Leo. Both of these are fire signs, which means that the ardent temperament and tempestuous history of this city is a reflection of elemental fire.

The interior of the mosque at Cordova, where both Christians and Muslims worshipped but at different periods. Cordova is ruled by Gemini, which is under the influence of the planet of communications, fleet-footed Mercury.

The fact is that one who is sensitive to such things can sense the zodiacal atmosphere of a place. For example, it is difficult to stand anywhere in the old part of Florence without feeling the impetuous mood of Aries, governed by the aggressive Mars. Florence is situated in a country ruled by creative Leo, the sign which rules the heart within the human body; and this is one reason why it became the artistic heart of the Renaissance. It is not surprising that one senses Florence to be filled with an inner dynamic power, an inner fire which fed European life and civilization for so many centuries. Again, Cordova in Spain is ruled by Gemini: no doubt the medieval Christians and Muslims who used the same ancient building there for worship (but at different times) were aware of the Geminian urge to relate harmoniously certain polarities within the soul. Gemini is ruled by Mercury, which in turn rules over astrology; so it is no surprise that, in the medieval period, Cordova was one of the main European centres for study of the stellar arts. As a further example we may take London, technically ruled by Gemini, a sign that certainly reflects the important duality of the place – divided into the City, the business centre, and Westminster, the political centre. The rapid pace of London life is typical of fast-moving Gemini, itself ruled by fleet-footed Mercury. Occultists regard it as no accident that the huge doors of the Bank of England, in the heart of the city, bear large images of the god Mercury, and that very many of the symbols within the city display, perhaps unconsciously, a Mercurial flavour.

The skyline of London. London is one of the few cities in the world to have a dual rulership. Some occultists say that the City, defined for astrological purposes as that area to the east of St Paul's, is ruled by Capricorn, and that part to the west is ruled by Gemini.

4 Heavenly and Earthly Lines

IN the second century AD, the Egyptian astrologer Ptolemy, using a system of calculation which is no longer part of modern astrology, determined that Spain was ruled by the zodiacal sign Sagittarius. There is some ground for accepting this rulership as valid, and a few authorities have insisted that the Sagittarian image of the archer-horseman finds its expression in the national literary hero Don Quixote. His bronze statue and that of his staunch follower Sancho Panza are the centrepiece of the lovely Plaza d'Espana in Madrid. The crazed hero, doting on knight-errantry and intent on redressing the wrongs of the world, may indeed be associated with the courtly and dignified fire sign Sagittarius; for the sign's prime concern is the regenerative effort to introduce spirit into matter, especially through endeavour in such fields as education and social reform.

In the days when Ptolemy suggested the Sagittarian rule over Spain, the sign was not represented by a horseman-archer but by a centaur (half-horse, half-man), an image interpreted by many as symbolising Man's emergence from the bestial state through self-discipline and spiritual aspiration. This Sagittarian centaur was associated with Chiron, a mythological figure skilled in hunting, medicine, music and prophecy who taught many of the Greek heroes. The Sagittarian bowman, whether human or centaur, aims his arrow at the skies, the perennial symbol of the spiritual realm, and prays that he may rid himself of his bestial and earthly nature: he is, like Chiron, an essentially practical type. While Cervantes's knightly hero certainly dreams and aspires, he is, to say the least, an impractical man – so inept, indeed, that his very name has become synonymous with the accident-prone idealist. Whatever the full nature of the Sagittarian, it is certainly far too practical and realistic a sign to be properly described as 'quixotic'.

Not surprisingly, some modern astrologers reject the notion of Spain as a Sagittarian country. They point out that though the land is peopled by a race of individuals who – while attached to the earth – are full of energy, exuberant joy and creativity, large areas of the country are tantamount to desert, something quite foreign to the notion of Sagittarius. In fact, there is nothing sacrosanct about Ptolemy's classification of countries and cities in terms of the signs of the zodiac. For example, his near-contemporary Manilius, a poet who wrote the five books of *Poeticon Astronomicon* in the reign of Augustus, insisted that Spain was governed by the dour earth sign Capricorn.

Those astrologers who reject both Sagittarius and Capricorn as ruler of Spain suggest that a more appropriate sign is the heavy and earthly Taurus, whose symbol is the celestial bull. A great deal of support for this Taurean rulership is provided by the fact that Spain's national sport is not that of tilting at windmills, but of baiting and killing specially-trained bulls. It is claimed by some scholars that this sport is the degenerate form of a religious ritual practised in ancient times. It involved, they argue, worship of the bull, and had its origins in the sacred initiation cults of the ancient Egyptians and, later, Cretan death-cults, from which stems the myth of the bull-headed monster of the labyrinth. Some authorities have even traced the brand-marks used to identify the bulls, which are sometimes found painted on the walls of bullrings, back to symbols used in the ancient hermetic art of alchemy. (Alchemy, in turn, was said to have its origin in Egyptian occult thought.)

Certainly, in earlier times, adepts in the astrological tradition recognised the importance of Egyptian and Cretan mythologies in the imagery of Taurus, and this explains why the bull has survived in the symbolism of many European cathedrals. The fact that the landscape of modern Spain is littered with gigantic images of bulls, sited in choice positions on hills in country and urban districts, also supports this notion that the country's nature is linked with the sacred bull. Thus the literary 'type' with which Spain might more reasonably be associated is Quixote's squire, Sancho Panza, a short, pot-bellied rustic, the very representative of the no-nonsense, faithful and earthly Taurean. Quixote, perhaps, is the type of Sagittarian and Sancho Panza the type of Taurean, so supporting another theory which suggests the courtly aristocracy of Spain may be linked with Sagittarius, while the peasant classes may be linked with Taurus.

There is a sense in which Spain introduced the occult lore of the ancient world to modern Europe, for during the Dark Ages almost all the occult tradition had been lost

Overleaf: **Mont St-Michel in northern France.**

Details of a series of sigils painted on the walls of a bullring. Such sigils are extremely ancient, and perhaps once had a secret significance relating to the esoteric background to bull-dancing and bullfights.

Below: the rulership of Taurus over Spain has been argued by many astrologers since it is very much an 'earthy' country (Taurus is an earth sign) and because the landscape is filled with images of bulls, from bull-fight posters to these gigantic figures set on prominent sites.

elsewhere. In Spain, however, it flourished during the period when the Moors, with their ancient magical lore and science, held the country. Arabic culture had always been fascinated by the magical traditions of alchemy and astrology, and it was largely through the Islamic courts and universities in Spain – especially from such places as Toledo and Segovia – that the occult lore of the ancient world, preserved and transformed by Arabic learning, was made available to the rest of Europe. Merged with this 'Spanish' Arabic occult learning were the esoteric traditions of the Jews, an extensive and powerful community in such cities as Segovia and Toledo. The secret traditions of their Cabbala, with its sophisticated occult teaching associated with, demonology and astrology, had the greatest influence on the development of European occultism. The powerhouse for such studies was the city of Toledo, where an estimated 12,000 Jews lived during the thirteenth century.

The flowering of this esoteric tradition was under Alfonso the Wise (1226–84) who took many of the leading exponents of Jewish magic as his own teachers and advisers. This enlightened patronage explains why Spain became the centre of occult learning in the medieval period, at a time when the rest of Europe had nominally rejected occult lore at the insistence of the Catholic Church. Europe as a whole was indebted to the scholarly research conducted in Spain, research disseminated by a stream of manu-scripts carried along the pilgrimage and trade routes. The fact is that the ancient astrological lore of the Greeks and Romans was reintroduced to medieval Europe through translations of Arabic and Jewish texts made in Spain. It is even claimed that the secret of paper manufacture (a Chinese invention, known to the Arabs through trade links with the East) was passed to Europe via Spain – a manufacture which alone permitted the later invention of printing in Germany. Once printing had been introduced to the other main European cities, a flood of books dealing with magic, astrology and occult lore was unleashed, and the ancient learning of Spain was rapidly absorbed by all the civilised nations of Europe.

In medieval times, when Europe was learning from its enemies the Saracens much of their ancient esoteric and occult lore, Toledo with its rich Jewish culture that maintained a high level of scholarship in the Cabbala (the secret lore of the Hebrews), as well as in magic and astrology, was one of the most important centres.

The infamous Inquisition, intent on putting a stop to heresy and witchcraft, did much to root out the practice of occult lore in Spain, but perhaps the deathblow to the study of magic and cabbalistic tradition was the pogrom against Spanish Jews in 1391 followed by their expulsion in 1492. The power of the Inquisition was such that the open study of magic, astrology and related arts was banished from all but the most secret conclaves in Spain. The study of occultism there appears to have been restricted mainly to the royal court and aristocratic circles, both of which were to some extent immune to the Inquisition's power.

PHILIP II AND THE ESCORIAL

As late as the sixteenth century, we find the Spanish king Philip II and many members of his court still actively encouraging the study of occult lore and astrology, and it is this survival from the past which accounts for the strange fact that the design and symbolism of one of that century's most remarkable buildings were rooted in magical and astrological lore. That building is the exquisitely proportioned El Escorial, to the north-west of Madrid, which was completed in 1584. On the orders of Philip, it was to serve during his life as his monastery-palace and, after his death, as his mausoleum.

The idea for the Escorial had come to Philip when his armies beat the French at St Quentin on 10 August 1557, the day of St Lawrence (*San Lorenzo* in Spanish). This is one reason why Philip dedicated the Escorial to San Lorenzo, and why, some insist, it is laid out in the form of a gridiron. (The gridiron is this martyr's symbol for he was roasted to death upon one.) It is said that the Escorial is orientated to sunset on 10 August, the feast of St Lawrence, so that its direction recalls not only the martyrdom of the saint but also Philip's victory at St Quentin. This explains why the façade of the building receives the early rays of the sun every day of the year, its austere and somewhat rigid lines softened by the warm glow. Similarly, it is surely no accident that the statue of Philip II in the

The Escorial is one of the few buildings in Spain to have been erected entirely according to occult and esoteric principles. The Spanish King, Philip II, was a student of magical and astrological lore, and designed the Escorial as a palace, monastery and mausoleum.

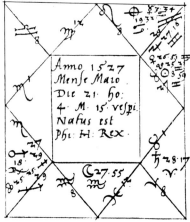

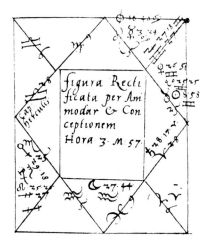

The two horoscopes cast for Philip II by the official court astrologer Sumbergius. At the top is the one cast for the actual moment of birth, as recorded by astrologers, while at the bottom is the rectified, or adjusted, chart cast long afterwards in the light of events which had occurred in Philip's life.

garden to the south-west is so placed that it faces the rising sun.

Though the idea arose from the events of a specific day, Philip certainly ensured that the building was built and orientated to a specific astrological moment, thus relating it to the cosmos (or at least to the zodiac) for all time. He had horoscopes cast to determine the best moment to begin the construction of the monastic palace, even regulating the three main phases of the building (palace, monastery and church) to different stellar conditions. This is not surprising, for there was a tradition in European architecture that important buildings should in some way express cosmic principles, and the most obvious way to do this was to ensure that the start of work on a building should be at a time harmonious with the planets and stars.

It is also clear that many surviving details of the building are directly related to Philip's personal horoscope, some of them so subtle as to have escaped the attention of scholars. He was born with the Sun in Gemini, and two horoscopes for his time of birth have survived. They are derived from the chart cast by Philip's official astrologer, Matthias Hacus Sumbergius, the originals of which are now preserved in the Royal Palace at Madrid. The published interpretation of these horoscopes, called the Prognosticon, is preserved alongside them. Other horoscopes cast for the King are recorded by the Italian astrologer Luc Gauricus, and the English magus-Rosicrucian John Dee, Queen Elizabeth I's astrological advisor, whom Philip had met in England during his ill-fated marriage to Mary Tudor.

No one has two valid horoscopes, of course, since a genuine horoscope merely maps out the positions of the zodiac, planets and stars at the moment of birth, and is therefore unique. Philip had two charts because the original was simply not regarded as sufficiently accurate, and was therefore 'rectified', or corrected, by Sumbergius after examination of the first chart. This rectification was made according to complex astrological factors, the most important of which was determining precisely the moment of conception. (This, supposedly, is reflected exactly in the birth chart.) The difference in the two charts is very slight indeed, involving only a matter of about eight minutes, but this lapse of time was sufficient to affect one or two very important elements within the original horoscope. For a start, the first chart gave Philip a Scorpionic ascendant, whereas the corrected chart moves it back two degrees to give him a Libran one. Thus, in adjusting the chart by only a few minutes, it was possible for the astrologer to give Philip a quite different astrological type.

That Philip recognised the validity of this corrected horoscope is borne out both by what we know of his character and by some of the more unfortunate events in his life. The correction, though minute, has the effect of putting the malignant planet Saturn exactly on the cusp of his seventh house, that house related directly to relationships and marriage, so affording Saturn greater importance than in the uncorrected chart. A person with Saturn so placed can hardly expect to have a happy relationship with those of the opposite sex, and the sad history of his four wives' deaths is testimony to this power of the planet. Some historians admit that Philip himself recognised the malign importance of Saturn in his life, and even go so far as to explain his preference for wearing black as a recognition of the importance of this planet (the only one of the seven to rule this colour). His melancholic disposition, even the madness which led him to rehearse his own funeral in the vaults of the Escorial, have been explained by astrologers in terms of the dark planet's influence.

If one accepts that the rectified horoscope is the genuine one, reflecting most accurately the precise moment of Philip's conception, then there is a further important change which must be taken into account. The fact is that the new Libran ascendant puts a powerful fixed star, called *Caput Herculis*, exactly on the important ascendant degree. For Sumbergius, this fixed star is of such momentous significance that he goes to the trouble of writing its name over the Ascendant point, so that even one not familiar with horoscope charts cannot fail to note its importance in the geniture. However, we should observe that during the sixteenth century there were over 60 important fixed stars which were often related to important points in the individual horoscope charts, and *Caput Herculis* was not regarded as being of sufficient importance to be listed among these. Clearly, there is some sort of mystery attached to the importance accorded this star by Sumbergius. For what reason does he single out this relatively unimportant star and accord it such an important influence on the chart of his royal horoscope?

In the sixteenth century, fixed stars played a much more influential role in astrology than in modern times, and we might therefore easily miss the significance of this new relationship between the Libran ascendant and Hercules had Sumbergius not drawn attention to it. Indeed, one gets the impression that it is mainly to introduce *Caput Herculis* that the chart was corrected in the first place. Could it be that it was inserted in order to indicate that, symbolically at least, Philip might be equated with the classical mythology of Hercules?

The constellation of Hercules, sometimes called 'The Kneeler' after the name used in Greek and Roman astrology, is said to have been placed in Heaven to commemorate the outcome of a battle. It is said that in the earliest days the Gods and the giants were at war, and in the course of their mightiest battle the huge and heavy race of giants all fled to one side of the heavens, which would have tipped over had not Atlas and Hercules supported them until the battle was over. Stellar mythology insists that Hercules was commemorated among the stars in honour of this deed. Perhaps the symbolic importance of this attempt to associate Philip with the starry Hercules lies in his having saved Spain against France at St Quentin; the suggestion being that he too was worthy of being placed in heaven.

This theory is almost certainly correct, for there is further confirmation of the importance of the Herculean image inside the Escorial itself. Philip had supervised every detail of the building's construction, but he took a special interest in the design and decoration of its library. This is only to be expected, for among its most important rulerships the significant planet Saturn is given power over philosophy, and it was in libraries that the activities of the philosophers and savants were most intently pursued. Philip ensured that every detail of this building, from the type of wood used for the bookcases to the paintings which decorated the walls and ceiling, should express the symbolism of the secret philosophies of all times. In addition, he ensured that among the books he presented to this new library were titles which would establish the Escorial as one of the most important collections of esoteric and hermetic books in Europe. On his orders, the library ceiling and wall frescoes were executed according to an esoteric and occult plan, and time and time again they include references to astrology and horoscopes (including constellations and fixed stars) along with portraits of such ancient astrologers and astronomers as the Persian Alchabitius, Ptolemy, and the patron of Spanish occult lore, Alfonso the Wise.

Of particular interest however, is the fact that on the eastern wall, which of course corresponds to the area where the ascendant (and the Sun) rises, is a somewhat unconventional picture of Hercules. This fresco, painted by Tibaldi and Carducci as part of the library's complex astronomical-astrological symbolic programme, shows Hercules in the role of *Hercules Gallicus* (the 'Gallic Hercules'), carrying a club in his right hand, a bow in his left, a lion's skin draped over his head and back, and a ball at his feet. From his mouth emerges a number of golden chains each of which run to the mouths of men who are apparently listening to him. In medieval lore, a golden chain was a symbol for secret wisdom, and many of the occult texts refer to a series of hermetic symbols depicting stages of being from the highest godhead down through the created realms to Man, and even lower into the realms of animals and demons. This series of hermetic symbols was called a golden chain, and we may therefore assume that the golden chains which bind Hercules to the other men are in some way connected with the secret lore; we may presume that Hercules is instructing those bound to him in some arcane lore or other secret knowledge. If this Hercules does indeed represent Philip, then we may take it that the King himself is regarded as the repository of a secret lore and occult knowledge which he is prepared to offer to other men by way of instruction.

The title Gallic Hercules is something of a mystery, for the hero is rarely called by his name. However, when performing his tenth labour he did penetrate into Gaul, and some claim that the triple-bodied monster Geryon (whose cattle he had to herd) reigned over the western coast of Iberia, which now includes Spain and Portugal, and over which (from 1580) Philip also had sway. Could this title be an attempt to link the Hercules of mythology – at least in the guise in which he visited Spain – with the

An example of a chain of sigils within the tradition known as 'The Golden Chain of Homer' (in Latin, *Aurea Catena Homeri*), showing the descent from the higher realms of heaven, through the astral plane, then through the etheric plane, into the realm of man, and even lower.

Aurea Catena Homeri.

Annulus Platonicus.

Superius & Inferius Hermetis.

Chaos	confusum.
Spiritus Mundi vo-	latilis incorporeus.
Spiritus Mundi	acidus corporeus.
Spiritus Mundi fixus	alcalicus corporeus.
Materia prima o-	mnium corporum
sublu-	narium.
Ani-	malia.
Vegetabilia,	seu Azoth.
Mine-	ralia.
Spiritus Mundi con-	centratus fixus seu
Extractum Chao-	ticum purum.
Perfectio consum-	mata, seu QuintaEs-
sentia Uni-	versalis.

Above: personification of
Astrologia, with the mercurial
caduceus in her hands. A detail
from the vast programme of
esoteric lore painted in fresco in
the library of the Escorial.

Another detail from the Escorial
library frescoes, showing an
astrological device, which makes
use of the fall of the sun on to a
triangular gnomen.

Spanish king? If so, then the Gallic Hercules is Philip himself, who (France excepted) had rule over many parts of Europe which had belonged to the ancient Gauls. The constellation of Hercules was regarded by the medieval astrologers as being one of those stellar patterns which would give victory in war, and many magical amulets and charms were inscribed with this figure (or its various symbols) for soldiers to wear on their campaigns.

Even though the entire constellation was involved with astrological and magical lore relating to success in warfare, the star known as *Caput Herculis* (as indicated on Philip's horoscope) was rarely regarded as being important. In fact, in Philip's day it would have been known as 'Ras Alheti' from the list of stars named in the Alfonsine tables which were constructed on the orders of Alfonso the Wise, and are still preserved in the Escorial library. Could we take it, therefore, that what is important in the horoscope chart is not so much an astrological as a symbolic matter? In the mythological stories, Hercules is identified with Hermes, and with Hermes's ability to charm men with the power of his words. This is surely the important element in the fresco depicting men chained to the mouth of Hercules, for the golden chain is nothing but words of secret wisdom.

Hercules had learned the art of music and singing, and this is the reason why he was so often identified with the Greek sage Hermes, who was the guardian of the sacred and secret wisdom. It is possibly this role, as initiate guardian, which is intended in the painting of the golden chains, for they suggest that Hercules is imparting his wisdom only to his followers, chaining them by the wisdom of his speech which would have no meaning for others.

There is also one other strain of hermetic symbolism in the Gallic Hercules figure. In his important text on stellar wisdom, Ptolemy said that the entire figure of the Hercules constellation (which he had called by its Greek name, *Engonasi*, 'The Kneeler') was of an influence similar to Mercury. This meant that the astrologer Sumbergius, who noted the importance of the constellation and fixed star in Philip's chart, was intent on pointing to the power of an additional Mercury in the King's life. Philip, like every one else, already had a Mercury in his chart (in his case, in the sign Cancer), but according to Ptolemy's dictum, the presence of the *Caput Herculis* evoked a second Mercury by virtue of the power of this star. Now this reference is of an occult nature. Mercury was the Roman name for the Greek god Hermes, who was the patron of magic, of the secret lore which had been bequeathed to the Greeks from Egypt and Babylon. The very word hermetic is from the name Hermes, and means secret or hidden. The horoscope therefore refers to something which is secret and hidden in the life of Philip, and clearly points to him as a man of extraordinary wisdom with the power of the ancient initiate over words, wisdom and man. The occult tradition lauded Hermes as Trismegistus (thrice blessed) because of his triple power as philosopher, king and priest. In demonstrating the double role of Mercury in Philip's chart, Sumbergius is surely suggesting that Philip is almost of the rank of this most powerful of all ancient initiates for he is at least 'twice blessed' as philosopher and king.

We have glanced at only one theme relating Philip's horoscope to a single symbol in one of the library frescoes. It is very likely that all 12 of the main frescos which decorate the walls each carry some significant symbolism relating to the 12 zodiacal signs in the horoscope of the king, and that the ceiling paintings, which depict the seven liberal arts (which are linked with the traditional symbolism of the seven planets) relate to the planets as they are evinced in Philip's personal horoscope.

This interpretation of the horoscope and the related frescoes in the Escorial library is not fanciful, for it is now recognised by scholars that part of Philip's plan was to make his palace incorporate something of the geometric symbolism of the famed Temple of King Solomon, a structure which had fascinated Jewish and other occultists for centuries. There is no doubt that the King's constant companion, the occultist and architect Juan de Herrera (who completed the design of the Escorial and even set down most of its decorative programme) was a learned esoteric, a devoted follower of the hermeticist Raymond Lully of Majorca, and widely read in magical and astrological lore. Philip instructed him to so lay out the building so that it would become a repository of arcane lore – perhaps, indeed, the most occult of all buildings in Spain.

MORE ZODIACAL SYMBOLISM

As we have seen in chapter 3, zodiacal symbolism in fresco paintings played an enormous part in medieval Italian programmes: this is why the main decorative cycles of the Salone in Padua, the Palazzo Chiericati in Vicenza, the Palazzo di Shifanoia in Ferrara, and the Villa Farnesina in Rome contain esoteric astrological symbols of a most important kind. The Villa Farnesina is based around the horoscope of Agostino Chigi, and was painted by Baldassare Peruzzi. This horoscope is probably the largest in the world, and is found on the ceiling of the Sala di Galatea. Besides the usual complement of zodiacal and planetary images, it contains over 18 constellations, no doubt with the intention of portraying with some accuracy the sidereal time in Rome at the moment of Chigi's birth. The form of the constellations of the Great Wain, Aquarius, Pegasus and Perseus represent the all-important Ascendant, which in the sixteenth century was usually called the *Horoscopos*. A reading of the indications set out in this vast chart suggest a birth time of 5.00 p.m., local time, on 1 December 1466.

In some cases, the orientation towards stellar points is intended to make use of the fact that the sun will throw rays of light through apertures and draw patterns on the earth, or, when directed towards specially calibrated lines, mark out the passage of time. The simplest use which is made of these solar rhythms is the sundial, but in some European cities large-scale solar calendars have been constructed around the orientation points marked by the sun as it appears to move around the earth. Probably the largest of these calendars is the one constructed by Cassini in San Petronio, in Bologna in 1655. The fall of the sun's rays through the roof aperture cuts various symbolic patterns on the columns – most notably the heart-shapes – but each day (the sun being in evidence, of course) a small circle of light will fall upon a calibrated strip to indicate the date and position of the Sun in the zodiac. In Bergamo a smaller but still impressive version of such a calendar has been built beneath the massive arches of the Palazzo della Ragione in the Citta Alta, and its calibrations and zodiacal sigils have been restored in recent times. Its setting must be one of the most lovely in all Italy, for it permits a view of the octagonal Baptistry by Giovanni da Campione, with the inset Virtues in red marble, the extraordinary Colleoni Chapel, designed by Amadeo in the fifteenth century, and the Church of Santa Maria Maggiore.

A far earlier use of solar orientation may be found in the Salone at Padua, within the walls of which is a veritable repository of occult lore. Among the 666 frescoes, most of which have an astrological or arcane theme, we find a simple porthole which permits sunbeams to enter at certain times of the day in the manner of ancient orientation systems. This porthole has been especially embellished with the gilded image of the Sun and linked with eucharistic symbols. Originally the sunbeams were directed towards a metal or marble strip on which the days of the year, and the corresponding zodiacal sigils were cut, but unfortunately this calibration has been removed and only vestiges of the original layout may be traced on the floor.

In contrast, the rich series of orientations which were set up in 1207 in the basilican church of San Miniato al Monte, Florence, are perfectly preserved, and may be studied each year. In this church, the marble zodiac (according to a nearby inscription, also laid down in 1207) is orientated so that Taurus, a symbolic representative of the Logos Christ, is directed towards the arc of daily sunrise over Florence. Far more dramatic, however, is the fact that the church structure is so orientated that twice each year a beam of sunlight falls from a high window to rest for a few seconds upon a fish symbol, set in marble on the wall of the raised choir. This is an arcane reference to the Resurrection of Christ in his role as leader of the Age of Pisces, the symbol for which is a pair of fishes.

Perhaps the oldest of zodiacal orientations involving beams of sunlight falling through specially placed holes is that in Externsteine, near Detmold, in Germany. Here, the orientation point is set extremely high in a chapel perched near the top of one of these distinctive rocks. The position of the chapel on the height of the rocks is such that, when viewed through the porthole, the hilly horizon appears level with the chapel itself so that on a certain day (the summer solstice of the 22 June) the first sunbeams are thrown through the porthole, parallel to the floor of the chapel, to cut a circle of light in the centre of the alcove at the back of the chapel. The purpose of this orientation is no

A detail showing how a shaft of sunlight falls from an upper window and sweeps through the interior of the basilica of San Miniato al Monte, in Florence, to light up the image of a fish on the altar wall.

Opposite: the zodiacal clock at Bergamo is a reproduction (with very few changes) of the medieval system designed to record the passage of the sun through the zodiacal arcs, and thus gives a permanent calendar.

The fourteenth-century mosaic showing Christ enthroned between the Virgin and San Miniato, in the church of San Miniato al Monte. The basilica has been so orientated, and the mosaic so designed that twice a year a beam of sunlight falls on Christ's foot, reaffirming the connection between Christ and the sunlight, and recalling the fact that zodiacal Pisces (the Fish) rules the human feet.

The zodiac in the nave of San Miniato al Monte, in Florence, which is the only dated marble zodiac in Europe. It was constructed when the present church was built, in 1207, and is one of the last remaining examples of an integral hermetic design in a medieval church, its symbolism being linked with daily and annual sunlight effects.

longer known, but it is possible that some ritual connected with this important solar position was enacted during the few seconds each year when this solar lighting took place. Some historians relate the chapel to early Mithraic mysteries, favoured by the Roman armies; but such mysteries, while undoubtedly using zodiacal imagery and orientation points relating to the sun, were usually enacted in underground chambers – a notable survival of which is found in the crypt of San Clemente in Rome. Those who seek to limit the rituals of the Externsteine to early Germanic mythology have suggested that Wodan was worshipped in this chapel, while the Roman historian Tacitus recorded that, according to the Germans, a prophetess lived in the upper sanctuary – it could be that she was involved in some way with the annual light effect. A more likely interpretation of the Externsteine site is in terms of the pagan symbolism built around the Irminsul tree (see page 116), but little is now known about this ancient mystery.

Orientation points are not always zodiacally directed, for sometimes they are related to significant places which have nothing to do with stellar symbolism, and everything to do with earthly symbolism. One of the most outstanding examples of this may be seen in the Piazza dei Miracoli, in Pisa, where the symbolic direction is linked to the medieval symbolism of the bull. The ground plan of the piazza shows three main buildings – the circular baptistry, the cruciform plan of the cathedral itself, and the famous Leaning Tower which is the campanile (bell-tower) for the cathedral. These three buildings are connected by secret symbolism.

Inside the baptistry is a pulpit designed around 1260 by Nicola Pisano. The symbolic device of the lectern makes use of established medieval symbolism and invites us to look for the image of a bull (symbol of St Luke, and of zodiacal Taurus) which should be on the pulpit, but which is missing. In other examples of this symbolism (which we find, for example, in the church at Grópina, and in San Miniato al Monte, in

The upper chapel which has been cut into the solid rock at Externsteine. At the summer solstice the light of the rising sun is thrown horizontally through a porthole in the projecting rock (to the right) and falls as a circle of light on the flat wall above an altar. It is likely that in former times this circle of sunlight fell upon some votive object, placed on the altar table. In this picture, which was taken before the solstice, the beam of light falls on the rock face some inches to the right of the altar wall.

The bull which juts out from the south-eastern wall of the duomo at Pisa is one part of a complex system of esoteric symbolism, linked with orientation lines which unite the baptistry, the cathedral and the Leaning Tower.

Florence) we find this hidden bull somewhere within the building itself, and its position is somehow significant in terms of a deeper Christian symbolism. However, there is no trace of the missing bull inside the baptistry, and if we are to discover the deeper symbolism of the Piazza we must look outside. In fact, we are able to locate the image of a bull high on the south-east corner of the cathedral itself. Its curious position indicates that a line of direction is to be traced from the pulpit within the baptistry, upwards towards the outer fabric of the cathedral. When this line is completed, we find our line of vision projected further upwards towards the top of the leaning bell-tower. The deep significance of the missing bull now becomes evident, for in medieval lore the bull is linked with Taurus, which is further linked with the human throat, with the larynx and with sound. This is why the bull is sometimes adopted as a symbol of Christ in his role as the descending 'Logos', or Word. The sacrificial bull is also the Sacrificial Word. In the Pisa symbolism, we are carried from the inner word, which will be spoken from the pulpit, into the visible outer word of the bull's head on the church exterior, and then upwards into the invisible outer sound of the bells on top of the campanile.

STANDING STONES AND PATTERNS

It has long been recognised that many of the standing stones erected in ancient times were intended as 'foresights' to measure and record the movements of the heavenly bodies. The usual explanation for this is that agrarian societies had to be certain of periodicities relating to the Sun and Moon, which determined the right time to sow and reap. There was also a need to date properly, in cosmic terms, the various festivals which were an intrinsic part of social life. Occultists, however, take this explanation a step further and insist that the ancients, who still had a priestcraft with deep knowledge of cosmic realities, also needed to know with great precision the times of eclipse, sunrise and sunset, lunar rhythms and so on in order to relate more consciously to the cosmos. Certain magical acts, and certain forms of sacrifice, could be enacted only at precisely significant cosmic moments.

This approach was dictated by far more than a need to direct the timing of festivals, for it sprang from a realisation that the life of Man, as indeed the life of societies, was in no way divorced from the life and rhythm of the planets and stars. It was almost certainly a memory of this truth which made Greek builders orientate the Parthenon towards the star-group of the Pleiades (as was revealed by Penrose), and why many of the earlier Egyptian temples were directed towards specific fixed stars such as Sirius.

The Parthenon is said to be one of the world's most perfect buildings, with each detail linked in some way with cosmic and stellar phenomena to ensure that it was a fitting home for the goddess Athena. The researcher Penrose showed that the Parthenon was orientated to the star cluster of the Pleiades, which had an almost mystical significance in classical times.

The study of such orientations has gained much popularity in modern times, and the essential principles are now so widely recognised that even amateurs, with no profound knowledge of the spherical geometry involved in the study of precise orientations, may discover, by visual exploration and direct observation, such important alignments for themselves. The remarkable Thom – who has a greater knowledge of the cosmic geometry of ancient alignments and circles than any other man – has provided many diagrams revealing a complex tissue of solar and lunar alignments, suggesting that the ancients used sighting points, backsights and both natural and man-made fixed viewing points.

One of those who had little or no knowledge of spherical geometry, but was nonetheless interested in orientations, was Alfred Watkins. He came to the conclusion that there were many alignments in Britain which marked straight lines through the countryside, but which were not specifically related to the positions of solar, lunar or stellar rising or setting points.

Lockyer noted a similar alignment at the Boscawen-un circle in Cornwall, which (in 1480 BC) ran along an ancient track leading from the circle to an outlying stone, now called the Tresvannack Pillar, some distance away. A further line of stones, strung out over a distance of about three miles towards the south-east, was investigated by Lockyer who recognised one of them as marking the position of the November sunrise, from the fixed viewing point of the Boscawen-un circle. Such alignments, remarkable as they no doubt are, may be regarded as fairly standard, as there may be little doubt that the stone circles and other alignments were intended, among other things, to mark important stellar and solar points. However, what is remarkable about the Boscawen-un circle is the fact, recorded by John Michell, that when Lockyer made his survey of the Cornish circle the presence of a further four stones had not been established. These four stones extend the line towards the November sunrise in a dead-straight line, and are visible from one alignment to another. They have been erected with such precision that even on an Ordnance Survey map they chart a dead-straight line. Stellar and planetary orientations require only three points – a fixed viewing point, an alignment point and a marking point – to determine a given position. There is no need to extend these three over a distance of three to five miles into infinity, so to speak, as is the case with some orientations. The reasons underlying this approach to menhirs remain a mystery, but perhaps they are not concerned merely with orientations, but also with the transmission of cosmic or telluric energies, as some of the followers of Watkins have proposed.

The gigantic metal statue of Arminius (a German hero who fought successfully against the Romans) which Ernst von Bandel raised on the hillside near Detmold in the nineteenth century.

Watkins's original ideas had been relatively simple. He outlined a theory suggesting that the ancients had marked straight lines across the countryside by means of a series of recognised landmarks which were either artificial or natural topographical points. The most usual artificial markers were upright stones, or buildings, while the most frequently used topographical points were natural stones (usually on horizon lines), distinctive hills, and so on. Since pathways were often established between such points, the pathways, the 'Old Straight Tracks' as Watkins called them, also became integrated into the systems of straight lines running across Britain. According to Watkins, such tracks led for very many miles in straight lines, following orientation point after orientation point, connecting places of obvious interest to the ancients such as holy sites, wells, meeting places, stone circles, and so on.

Although a pioneer in this field, Watkins was not alone in seeking out orientation lines by means of natural and artificial structures between sacred sites. Wilhelm Teudt, a German fired by somewhat blinkered enthusiasm for the Teutonic past, also spent much of his life exploring orientation lines, deriving his first notions from study of the 'sacred heartland' of Germany, the rock towers of the Externsteine, near Detmold. Teudt and his followers collected thousands of German 'leys' (orientations supported by distinctive markers, usually running in straight lines over great distances), and extended their researches into stellar orientations, similar in principle to the more learned Penrose. For example, Teudt regarded the old walls of the village of Osterholz as orientated according to stellar directions, the western wall being towards Cappella, the northern wall towards Sirius, one southern wall towards Orion, and another towards Castor. The eastern wall marked important lunar positions. Why such incredible complexities were necessary in the layout of a village – other than to demonstrate the superiority of the ancient Teutonic astronomy – is never adequately explained.

The stellar orientations of Osterholz may owe too much to Teudt's fevered brain, but much of his work on Externsteine was sound. It is almost a smaller version of that other sacred centre and religious sanctuary (adopted by Byzantine monks) – Meteora, in northern Greece. We may have no doubt that it has always been of great importance as a Teutonic religious centre. Even in pagan times, it was already well integrated into mythology, for we find it in the Scandinavian *Eddas*. In history it was the place where the Roman legions met defeat at the hands of the Teutonic tribes – an event immortalized in the magnificent Arminius statue near Detmold, by Ernst von Bandel. Later, following Goetheian romanticism, Externsteine was associated with specifically Teutonic folk culture, and in the early part of the nineteenth century it was recognised that the chapel's curiously-placed porthole, excavated into one of the rocks, was directed so as to admit the first sunlight at summer solstice, and to permit a view of the Moon at its northern extreme.

THE SACRED TREE

The most interesting survival of early Christian use of Externsteine as a cult centre is a relief carving of the Irminsul, the mystical German 'Tree of Life', itself linked with the great Nordic Yggdrasil tree. In the relief, this Irminsul is bowing down (symbolic of its recognition of the new mystery wisdom of Christianity) under the weight of one of the disciples as the body of the Christ is taken down from the cross. Above, to the left of the cross, is a weeping male personification of the Sun; to the right, a weeping female personification of the Moon, indicating that the sacrifice of Christ was of cosmic importance. Part of the significance of this Christian version of the Irminsul lies in the fact that it is contrasted with another 'tree' mythology which is part-carved, part-natural, on another of the Externsteine rocks. This one depicts Odin hanging on the tree in his attempt to attain inner wisdom.

The sacred tree finds its way into virtually every culture, and since the Cross upon which Christ died is one of the four Christian sacred 'trees', there is no awkwardness in a relief which represents one pagan tree bowing out in recognition of the might of a later one. Trees abound in sacred symbolism, and often have distinctive forms of attributes which serve to render them unique to a particular mythology. There are the Trees of Eden, the sacred palm tree of Apollo in Delos, the Asherah of Dodona in Epirus, the

The mystical and mysterious outcropping of rocks at Externsteine, which has become intimately linked with the myths and history of German nationalism and both pagan and Christian mysticism. The rocks have been carved to make grottoes, chapels, stairs, hermit cells, and even initiation chambers.

On one of the Externsteine rocks is an image of the Descent from the Cross, with symbols reminiscent of the Grail imagery, which include the pagan Irminsul, the sacred tree of the Teutonic mystery wisdom, bowing down to the new wisdom of Christianity.

Ficus Ruminalis of the Roman Palatine, the Bodhi-Tree of the Buddhists, the Tree of Dubhros in Irish mythology (which is guarded by the one-eyed magician-giant Searbhan), the two trees of Scandinavian mythology, the ash (from which the first man was made), and the elm (Embla) from which the first woman was made, as well as the familiar Tree, or cross, upon which Christ died and which, in popular medieval tradition, had been grown from a cutting of the Tree of Knowledge in the Garden of Eden.

To judge from the Irminsul on the Christian relief, the tree belongs to an ancient tradition and is linked with the Pythagorean Y, a symbolism which has survived into modern times in the shape of the divining rod made from a hazel twig. The Pythagorean Y is, among other things, a symbol of man's path through life, in which he is perpetually faced with two choices; one of these is the left-hand path leading to moral decay; the other is the right-hand path leading to moral perfection. Of course, the possibility is that, within this Christian context, the bent Irminsul is also intended as a reference to the tree from which the wood of the cross was made.

THE EARTH AND THE STARS

Perhaps the most daring of attempts to relate earth places to cosmic theory is that proposed by Charpentier in his study of Chartres. He shows that a study of the map of France, within a circumference of about 100 miles, reveals that the sites of the churches and cathedrals dedicated to the Virgin Mary correspond to the main stars in the constellation of Virgo. This correspondence, adapted from Charpentier's diagram, is reflected in the map, and shows the following relationship between stars and places:

The virgin places of northern France. The top map shows the star positions of the constellation Virgo, which some modern occultists claim is reflected in the place map of those churches and cathedrals dedicated to the Virgin (the heavenly Virgo) in northern France, between Laon, Chartres and Bayeux.

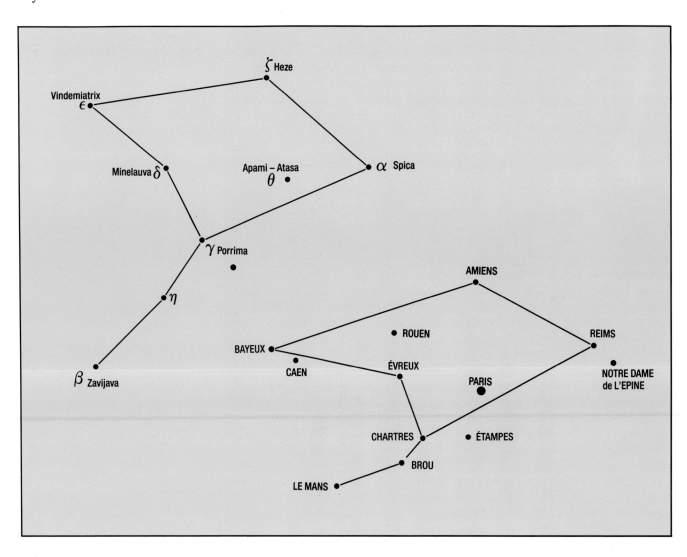

STAR NAME	MODERN DESIGNATION	FRENCH 'NOTRE DAME'
Reims	α (alpha) Virginis	Spica
Le Mans	β (beta) Virginis	Zavijava
Chartres	γ (gamma) Virginis	Porrima
Évreux	δ (delta) Virginis	Minelauva
Bayeux	ϵ (epsilon) Virginis	Vindemiatrix
Amiens	ζ (zeta) Virginis	Heze
(Brou)	η (eta) Virginis	(no modern name)
Paris	θ (theta) Virginis	Apami-Atasa*
Laon	(74) Virginis	(no modern name)

* A name recorded by R. H. Allen, *Star Names. Their Lore and Meaning,* (1963).

The fact that Reims heads the list, marking the brightest star in the constellation, is not surprising since this was the cathedral where Kings of France were traditionally crowned. The Latin name, *Spica*, means ear of corn, and in medieval imagery the ear of corn in the left hand of the sky Virgin was often visualised as being transformed into the Child Jesus (the bread who feeds Mankind) in the hands of the Virgin Mary. So closely were the constellation of Virgo and the Virgin related in popular thought that the thirteenth-century Albertus Magnus proposed that the sigil for Virgo, written ♍ was a drawing of MV, for Maria Virgo. The French for ear of corn is *L'Epi* and to the south-east of Reims a Notre-Dame de L'Epine (the last word means thorn and is a reference to the Crown of Thorns worn by Christ) has been built since the medieval period, when the other cathedrals were located. *Spica* has long been associated with important orientation points, and Lockyer records several examples of Egyptian temples which were directed towards its setting point. The only place on the map which does not appear to have a dedication to the Virgin is Brou.

The Latin *Vindemiatrix*, for the star linked with the position of Bayeux, means female grape gatherer, but in Roman times it was *Vindemiator* meaning male grape gatherer. (The name is said to derive from the fact that this star rises in the morning just prior to the gathering of the vintage.) One wonders if this change of name and sex was anything to do with the feminine nature of the Virgo constellation which the star marked?

The French researcher, Maurice Leblanc, was the first to observe that the Benedictine abbeys of the Caux country traced, in a similar way, the figure of the Great Bear constellation on the earth.

Relating to star patterns which connote connections derived from names (such as Virgo-Virgin) is one thing, but studying straight lines between places on modern maps is another. Much of the work done by Teudt in Germany was concerned with tracing *heilige Linien* (sacred lines) that were supposed to link churches and holy places by straight lines. The result is a series of parallel and rectilinear lines drawn upon maps which tell us a great deal about the Germanic concern for precision and very little about sacred places or ley lines. An example may be taken from the records made by Röhrig, following indications given by Teudt, of a *heilige Linien* survey in Ostfriesland, in which he claims to trace straight lines between three (or sometimes four) places, each with some 'sacred' connotation, such as a church. Rohrig draws a north-south line through the churches at Arle, Bangstede, Simonswolde, and Dorenborg, a line which en route passes through an island in the Ems.

The truth is that such orientation points are actually very easily discovered on maps, because the small scale of even large maps permits such a wide error (sometimes errors of miles, when reduced from scale to actual landscape). Additionally, when querying these *heilige Linien* surveys, one must also call into question whether the

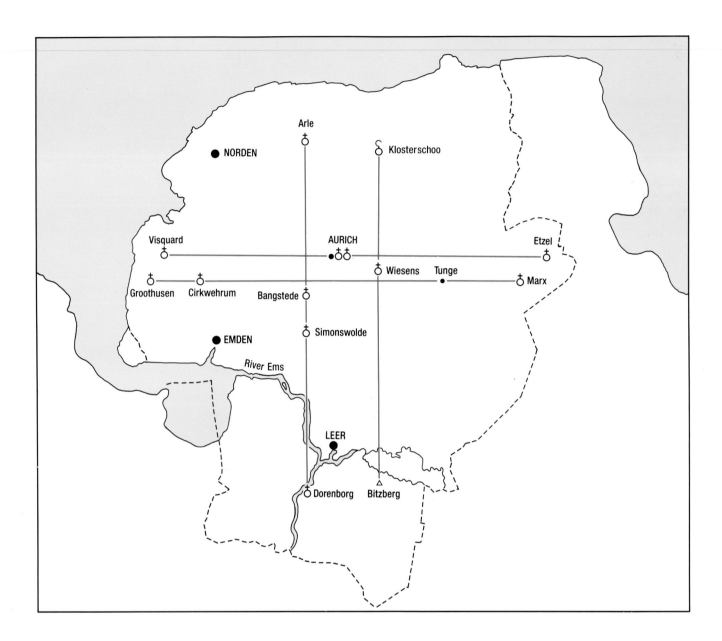

Four of the important ley lines traced by Röhrig in Ostfriesland. Röhrig's own maps were incredibly complex, and not always accurate.

methods of modern projection used in drawing up maps (and based on complex trignometrical systems) is similar to that observed by the ancients who founded or located the original sites. What may be viewed pragmatically as a straight line, determined by a series of observational points on an actual landscape, will not necessarily be a straight line on a map.

If we restrict ourselves to examining a supposed orientation point arising from Röhrig's own Ostfriesland, for example, we might (armed with a sufficiently long ruler and a good map) trace a single line moving from north to south from Altgarmssiel, through Barssel, Werlte, Wieste, Seppenrade to Olfe. Having done that, we must ask ourselves what purpose is served by having established such a line. If such a line may be drawn between points having no 'sacred' connections, then what purpose is served by drawing lines between points which have? Undoubtedly, there are such things as earth currents, and undoubtedly the old pilgrimage routes appear to have followed them (presumably on the basis that a pilgrim would be bathing himself in the revitalizing power of the earth while traversing such routes) yet all the evidence suggests that earth currents do not move in a straight line. Chinese *Feng Shui* experts, who have specialized in earth currents and related phenomena, call the currents 'dragon lines'; a term which evokes the sinuous curvilinear nature of such natural forces in a more convincing way than any of the rectilinear *heilige Linien* of Teudt and his school.

The method of orientation developed by Teudt has become popular in modern

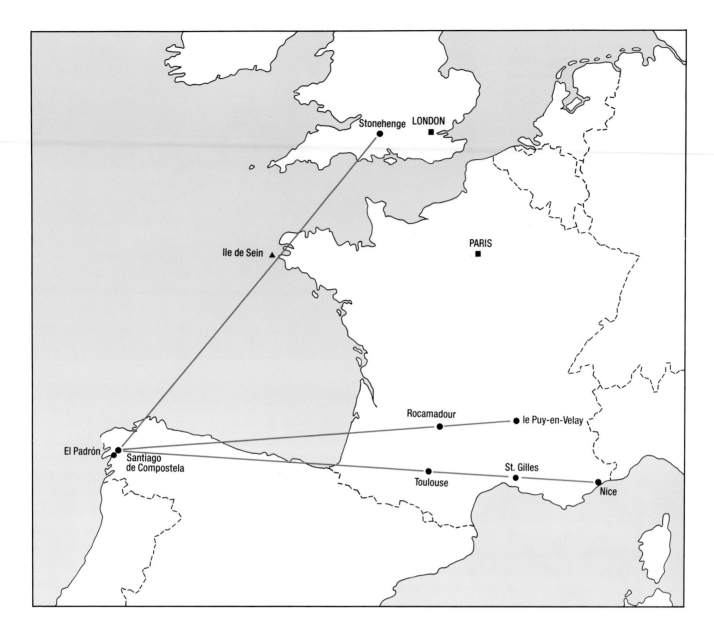

times, in spite of its unreliable basis, and many esotericists have proposed orientation lines – sometimes called 'Golden Chains' – linking together various places on maps in a manner which would have been quite foreign to the ancients. For example, the French writer Guy-René Doumayrou, taking the ancient Celtic city of Santiago de Compostela as an axis point and the great stone of El Padron as a marker, traces a straight line through the Ile de Sein (a Druidic centre) in the north-east (thus traversing the Bay of Biscay) as far as Stonehenge, in England. From the same Spanish city, he traces another line through the sacred site of Rocamadour in France through to Le Puy en Velay. Yet again, in revealing these 'Great Axes' of Compostela, he traces a line from the city, through Toulouse, St Gilles and Nice.

Another French writer on similar themes, Jean Phaure, points to some of the cathedral orientations of France – indicating, for example: that the cathedral at Chartres is directly on the line marking the setting of the sun at Winter solstice, and the rising of the sun at the Summer solstice; and that the Notre Dame at Reims is orientated on a line marking the setting of the Sun on the 1 November, and the rising of the Sun on the 15 August, the feast day of the Assumption of the Virgin. This latter orientation line appears to be reflected in the ancient Roman plan of the city, suggesting that, while obviously of Christian import in modern times, it was originally rooted in a pagan orientation. Phaure has also made a careful study of the orientations involved in that most remarkable of all French mystical sites, the Mont St-Michel. He indicates that the

The orientations associated with the Great Axes of Santiago de Compostela – the link between the Padron Rock, the Ile de Sein and Stonehenge – are extended to other ancient power centres by some modern occultists.

Mont St-Michel reflected in the early morning tide. The orientation lines include the directing of the abbey church on a south-west axis which reflects precisely the setting of the sun on 11 November and the 2 February. The church of St Pierre, to the east of the abbey church, is directed towards the sunrise on the 29 September.

Some of the most interesting ley lines linked with Paris, centred upon the Louvre, a name which some occultists derive from the alchemical word *l'oeuvre* (the Great Work). Some occultists claim that Montsouris is also connected with the Montmartre ley.

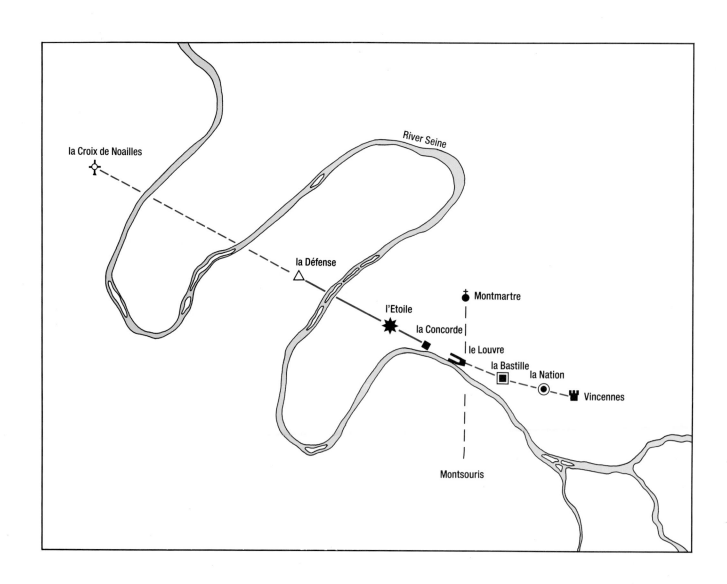

Abbey Church itself is directed in such a way as to reflect an earthly and stellar fiducial, since it is orientated south-west exactly towards Mont Dol, on a line which also marks the setting of the Sun on 11 November and 2 February. The Church of St Pierre, on the same mystic isle to the east of the Abbey Church, is orientated towards the rising of the Sun on 29 September.

Sometimes it is difficult to know what to make of all these outstanding orientation points. For sure, they do reveal quite convincingly that the ancients orientated their buildings in such a way as to establish a meaningful relationship to the stars, and thus to the Gods and angels who dwelled in the realm of the stars; but one must be wary of leaping to the conclusion that long-distance orientation lines have any significance, or that they reflect telluric, or earth currents, that they are, in short, representative of ley lines.

The truth is that Nature herself does not appear to produce straight lines, preferring spirals and curvilinear rhythms which are seemingly opposed to the rectilinear. One must not confuse the man-made with the natural; and there are few diagrams more revealing of this than the orientation now called the 'Axis of the Louvre'. Centred in Paris, and published in its original form by Doumayrou, the straight lines of orientation, based on man-made planning, cut through the meander lines of the Seine in a striking way, illustrating the contrast between the thinking of man, and the 'thinking' (or activity) of Nature. The contrast does not in any way demote the theory of Doumayrou, which traces an 'earth' orientation between the two mounts of Montsouris and Montmartre, in Paris, through the siting of the Louvre palace itself.

The interesting point raised by Doumayrou is that the origin of the word *Louvre* almost certainly lies in the fact that the secret Alchemy was called 'L'oeuvre' (the 'Work', or the 'Great Work'), and so the siting of the palace was probably linked with the esoteric tradition from which alchemy arose. We may be certain that the two orientation lines which derive from the Louvre point to stellar factors: to the north-west, we trace a straight line from the Louvre through Concorde, the 'star' of L'Etoile, the triangle of La Defense, as far as the Croix de Noailles. Each of these symbols (the star, the triangle and the cross) is in fact an esoteric symbol, possessing deep significance within the alchemical tradition.

To the south-east, we trace a similar line connecting the Bastille, La Nation, and the Château at Vincennes, which plays such an important part in esoteric history of French political and social life.

Vincennes would not be important in an orientation line of this kind were it not for its connection with alchemy. The place has gained for itself the reputation of being the most famous of all centres where royal 'black magic' was practised, for both Catherine de Medici and her son Henri III were reputed to be alchemists and magic-workers during their long stay there. It is claimed that Henri worked as an alchemist in either the Tour de Paris (a significant name, in view of the orientation involved) or in what is now called the Tour du Diable. Engravings made of the objects found in one of these towers after his death reveal nothing especially diabolical, however, except perhaps the statuettes of satyrs, which call to mind the god Pan, prototype of the European image of the Devil with his goat-horns and cloven hooves. If such objects were used for purposes of black magic, then the power exuded would have had to be obtained by 'reversal magic' – that is, by the reversing or inverting of the cross, or any other Christian objects, to demote and rechannel their energies. In the case of the statuettes, we might imagine the satyrs to have been placed in some lewd posture, perhaps standing on the reversed cross upon an altar. However, such considerations of 'reversal orientation' in black magic should not deflect us from sensing that Catherine and Henri were almost certainly interested in alchemy and, like the unfortunate Gilles de Rais (see page 71), who had a similar interest, gained for themselves reputations they did not deserve.

In the light of all this, we may grasp the importance of the invisible lines linking Vincennes with the Louvre, in Paris. It is, as Doumayrou suggests, true that the Louvre (the place of the 'Great Work') appears to mark the spiritual centre of Paris, rooted in the security of the earthly line of the two mounts, and projecting symbols in two grand directions which are themselves almost on the west-east axis of the world.

5 The Rosicrucians of Europe

THE original Rosicrucians were a secret fraternity who worked in various parts of Europe – though mainly in Germany. During the early part of the seventeenth century there was an enormous upsurge of interest in Rosicrucianism, which was long thought to mark the birth of the order. However, more recent research, supported by a collection of unique manuscripts preserved in Cologne, indicate that it may have more ancient origins. The vowed aim of the Rosicrucians was to prepare for the coming of a new Christian age, and their published literature was written from a quasi-occult and alchemical standpoint. At the centre of Rosicrucian belief was the idea that inner consciousness and power – even over death itself – can result from philosophical studies and intellectual development. The early symbols by which the Rosicurcians were identified were the image of the rose and cross (sometimes written as the Rosy + Cross) and the image of a red cross with a red rose. A typographical symbol was CRC, a reference to Christian Rosencreutz ('Christian Rose Cross'). Another Rosicrucian device (designed by the English magus John Dee) was a curious sigil called the 'Monas', which we shall examine later.

The movement attracted many important people – including, it is said, kings and emperors – and had a profound effect on the development of Europe. Long after the seventeenth-century flowering of Rosicrucianism, several other bodies – less secret in their organisation and rituals – established themselves and adopted various forms of the name Rose-Cross. For example, some of the nineteenth-century fraternities which were otherwise linked with the masonic movement, and which later flourished in France and England under the name of the Order of the Golden Dawn, were linked with the Rosicrucian school. There is still an extensive modern Rosicrucian movement, now centred in the United States, the published aims and literature of which link certain Rosicrucian principles with Steiner's Anthroposophy and Blavatsky's Theosophy. However, the majority of the original ideas and aims of the first Rosicrucians disappeared as mysteriously as they had begun.

Page 124–5: Heidelberg Castle, one of the most famous of all Rosicrucian centres in Europe.

The symbol for the Rosicrucians is based on a rose and a cross. In this image, derived from a book by the English Rosicrucian, Robert Fludd, the rose is carried on a thorn stem which is in the form of the cross. The Latin inscription, which is probably an acrostic of sorts, reads: 'the rose gives honey to the bees'.

Opposite: this plate, after a print by Michaelspacher, brings together many of the important themes of alchemy, including the seven grades (steps), the mystical cave where the operation takes place, the correspondences between the twelve signs of the zodiac and the twelve alchemical operations, and the importance of the four elements of Earth, Air, Fire and Water.

THE FIRST ROSICRUCIAN TEXTS

In the early seventeenth century, when the secret band of Rosicrucians decided to make their ideas public, they chose to direct their main thrust from Germany, where the art of printing was highly developed and where interest in alchemy and other occult streams of thinking was at its height. The Germans of the medieval period had been deeply influence by the influx of Arabic occult ideas, and many strange men (later quite rightly associated with the occult tradition) wandered through the land, studying and teaching various secret disciplines. Among these were Trithemius of Sponheim, the influential Swiss esotericist Paracelsus, and Agrippa of Nettesheim, whose classic book on medieval occult lore was to become the most important single influence in this field. In addition, Bohemia, the cultural life of which was intimately connected with that of Germany, had long been a centre for occult studies.

The earliest of the published Rosicrucian texts was probably written by Valentin Andreae of Württemberg. It is a mystical alchemical extravaganza about a royal wedding, *The Chymical Wedding,* and was first published in 1616. The book introduced

The occultist, esotericist and doctor of medicine, Paracelsus. He is holding the handle of his sword, in which he was supposed to have kept his azoth, the secret alchemical powder which was used both for transmutation and as an elixir of life.

A portrait of the occultist Agrippa von Nettesheim, from the title page of his most famous work, *De Occulta Philosophia,* which has had a profound influence on subsequent occult studies. Although written much earlier, the text was not published until 1532.

HENRICVS CORNELIVS AGRIPPA,

☞ Nihil est opertum quod non reueletur,
& occultum quod non sciatur.
Matthæi   X.

to the world the name of Christian Rosencreutz, the Christian Rose-Cross, who was to become the central figure of the Rosicrucian movement. The modern historian Frances Yates has suggested that Heidelberg castle was the real site of the strange emblematic castle mentioned in Andreae's *The Chymical Wedding*. In the days when the first Rosicrucian texts were published, Heidelberg was the home of the Elector Palatine, who appears to have been involved in the movement and who certainly surrounded himself with people specialising in arcane and occult lore. Both the interior and exterior of his medieval castle had been designed as a wonderland. The immense flat plateau which was used for the gardens had been blasted from the top of the rock behind the castle, and the landscape architect and engineer, Salomon de Caus, had constructed upon it a marvel of mechanical models, intricate pathways, mazes and amphitheatres. It was described by contemporaries as the eighth wonder of the world. In the gardens were mechanical fountains of great complexity and beauty, some of which would play music as they threw jets of water into the air. Chief among the marvels were the speaking statues, among which, for example, was a replica of the statue Memnon, of Egyptian fame, which sang when the rays of the early morning sun fell upon it. The mystical garden was completely destroyed in later centuries, but prints made in the 1620s give some idea of its magnificence. In the following century, it was still one of the favourite haunts of the great occultist Goethe, whose bust is mounted to the west of the garden.

The castle which was sited beside this remarkable garden was indeed reminiscent of the mystical castle (with its exotic garden) described by Andreae in terms intended to suggest that an occult relationship lay behind the physical appearance of the ordinary, familiar world. The giant statues of medieval knights in armour can still be seen, while the inner courtyard, flanked by the richly-decorated façades of the Friedrich Building and the later Ottheinrich building, has at the top the seven planetary statues which

A coloured engraving by Matthäus Merian showing a view of Heidelberg Castle, at the time when the gardens had been laid out according to occult and Rosicrucian principles by Salomon de Caus. To prepare the site for the garden, a large part of the hillside had to be removed.

One of the jars from the laboratory at Heidelberg Castle, which has been transformed in modern times into a pharmaceutical museum. The jar is marked with alchemical sigils denoting the nature of its original contents.

An alchemical oven and still, one of the most common pieces of apparatus used in the alchemical operation. In the museum at Heidelberg Castle a great deal of such equipment has been preserved, along with athanors and furnaces designed to give the different heats so important to the alchemical operation.

figure so frequently in Rosicrucian texts. The original statues, carved by Alexander Colin from Mecheln, have been replaced by modern copies in order to preserve them. Of special importance to those interested in esoteric and occult lore are the exhibits in the German Pharmaceutical Museum which is located in the cellar of the Ottheinrich building. Not only is there an important display of early herbal recipes and container jars, still bearing their ancient alchemical sigils, but also an extraordinary collection of the utensils, jars, furnaces, retorts, alembics and other distillation equipment used by both herbalists and alchemists in previous centuries. The cellar of the Apothecary's Tower, which has now been restored as a laboratory, was clearly used as an alchemical centre in earlier times.

This connection between Heidelberg castle and the alchemical fantasy of *The Chymical Wedding* has suggested to more than one historian that the Rosicrucians, for all their arcane, occult and alchemical symbolism, were at the front of a political movement aiming to bring about a religious revival within the Protestant realm. Yates leans towards the view that the Rosicrucian movement was rooted in a form of alliance between Protestant sympathisers who had gathered together in various German cities to counteract the Catholic League. A prophecy made in Simon Studion's *Naometria* predicted that the year 1620 would see the end of the 'reign of the Antichrist and the downfall of the Pope and Mahomet', after which, in 1623, the new millennium would begin. It is possible that his influential work lay behind a rash attempt made by Frederick, the Elector Palatine, to accept the Bohemian crown. This action, taken against the advice of his most astute advisors, resulted in his ruin and contributed to the start of the Thirty Years War which devastated Europe and virtually put an end to the original Rosicrucian school.

It is maintained by some esoteric scholars that the main creative force behind the Rosicrucian movement in Germany was the English magus (and sometime astrologer to Queen Elizabeth I), John Dee. As Yates points out, during Dee's long stay in Germany he met many esotericists who were to become involved in the later promulgation of Rosicrucianism. Indeed, in 1589, he journeyed through those same territories which, 25 years later, were to be the sites of the movement's outbreak. It is known that while in Bremen, Dee met the occultist Khunrath, and his considerable influence is evident in the latter's most famous work, *The Amphitheatre of Eternal Wisdom* (1609). Indeed, the second of the Rosicrucian manifestos, the *Confession* of 1615, was published alongside a Latin tract of Dee's own hermetic work on the magical sigil known as the Monas. (This became one of the standard symbols of the Rosicrucian movement, and almost as important as the famous Rose and Cross image. Dee's influence may also be noted in *The Chymical Wedding* of 1616, which includes upon its title page the very same Monas, perhaps with the intention of pointing to the Rosicrucians' esoteric origin.

This early stage in the promulgation of esoteric, alchemical and Rosicrucian ideas is now most easily studied through the lives and writings of a group of individuals who remain shadowy figures mainly because so little is known about them other than from the books they wrote, the illustrations they provided for their texts, and clues to the places where they lived and worked. Among them are Daniel Stolcius, Michael Maier, Daniel Mylius, Daniel Cramer and Heinrich Khunrath, most of whom were based in Frankfurt am Main, where the remarkable Johann Jennis was the most influential publisher of Rosicrucian and alchemical texts during the seventeenth century.

The publisher Jennis, who – through his printing activities and friendships with the leading alchemists and occultists of the day, turned Frankfurt am Main into a veritable centre for Rosicrucianism – is believed to have been a member of an esoteric group called the Family of Love, to which a large number of European publishers belonged during the seventeenth century. So exceptional was the talent of his chief engraver, Theodorus de Bry (also a member of the esoteric group), that when the English occultist Robert Fludd sought an engraver/illustrator for his *Utriusque Cosmi Historia*, he could find no one in England with equal knowledge of the secret tradition to execute the work, and so turned to the de Bry family, in Oppenheim. His choice resulted in some of the most famous of all occult illustrations (widely reproduced in esoteric texts and histories even today), designed mainly to illustrate the cosmic harmonies as they manifest themselves in the 'smaller world' of Man.

QVI NON INTELLIGIT, AVT TACEAT, AVT DISCAT.

IGNIS

AËR

MONAS HIEROGLYPHICA
IOANNIS DEE, LONDINENSIS,
AD
MAXIMILIANVM, DEI GRATIA
ROMANORVM, BOHEMIÆ ET HVNGARIÆ
REGEM SAPIENTISSIMVM.

DE RORE CÆLI, ET PINGVEDINE TERRAE, DET TIBI DEVS. Gen.27.

Guliel.Silvius Typog.Regius, Excud.Antuerpiæ, 1564.

The title page of John Dee's *Monas Hieroglyphica*. This magical sigil, reproduced in the central cartouche, is said to contain all esoteric lore. In essence, it consists of a mercurial caduceus, with a central dot set within the large circle, which is thereby made a solar sigil, the entire figure being mounted on a primitive sigil for Aries, which marks the beginning (and the end) of the zodiacal circle.

Whatever the historical reasons, a flood of alchemical and Rosicrucian works began to pour from the cities of Frankfurt and Leipzig in the early seventeenth century. This literature was read avidly, mainly because the curiosity and enthusiasm of the reading public had been aroused by the notion of secret fraternities which sought to change society by the application of Christian principles interpreted in the light of occult lore. In 1677, Frankfurt saw the publication of the second edition of what was, without doubt, the most important collection of alchemical Rosicruian tests produced in Europe – the *Musaeum Hermeticum* – of which only a few copies are still in existence. The entire series of 21 treatises, with their marvellous esoteric plates was produced by the de Bry family of engravers, and the Rosicrucian booksellers Luca Jennis and Matthäus Merian the elder. Perhaps the most extraordinary of these plates were those used to illustrate the last of the treatises, the *Janitor Pansophus*, which attempts to portray, in emblems and symbols, the entire basis of alchemical endeavour.

As is so often the case with alchemical and Rosicrucian works, the identity of the authors of some of these documents remains unknown, and this reminds us that the Fraternity was proud of the fact that its members were supposed to be 'invisible', or unrecognised. However, among the alchemical treatises was one by Basil Valentinus,

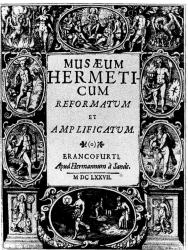

Title page of one of the most influential of alchemical-Rosicrucian texts, the *Musaeum Hermeticum*, published in 1677. The text is written by a number of different authors, most of them Rosicrucians, and many of the engravings are of superb quality.

A large hand-coloured engraving by Merian to illustrate a short text by Janitor Pansophus, included in the *Musaeum Hermeticum*, relating to the cosmic harmonies. This plate is ostensibly an illustration to the oldest known (and possibly apocryphal) alchemical text, *The Emerald Tablet* supposedly written by Hermes Trismegistus. It was reputed to contain all hermetic lore: the plate itself attempts to incorporate all the major symbols, sigils and graphic ideas, including the androgynes, the female-lunar and the male-solar, the conjunction of opposites, the divisions of the labours in the production of the philosopher's stone, and the nature of the cosmos (or macrocosm) which is visualised as a reflection of the lower world (microcosm).

All the plates reproduced on this page are from the *Musaeum Hermeticum*.

Right: the White Unicorn and the Red Stag, emblems of the alchemical process, are from the Lambsprinck text *De Lapide Philosophico (Concerning the Philosopher's Stone)*, published in Frankfurt in this edition in 1677.

Below right: the Green Ouroboros Dragon, devouring its own tail, is one of the recurrent alchemical symbols, which on one level represents the concept of cyclical time. The Green Dragon, however, is also one of the terms used to denote a certain alchemical process, a stage relevant to the making of the philosopher's stone.

Below: the title page of Lambsprinck's book, as reproduced in the *Musaeum Hermeticum*.

LAMBSPRINCK
*NOBILIS GERMANI PHILOSOPHI
ANTIQVI LIBELLVS*
De
LAPIDE PHILOSOPHICO,
*E Germanico verſu Latinè redditus, per Nicolaum
Barnaudum Delphinatem Medicum, hujus
ſcientiæ ſtudioſiſſimum.*

FRANCOFURTI,
Apud HERMANNUM à SANDE.
M DC LXXVII.

SUBTILIS ALLEGORIA
Super
SECRETA CHY-
MIÆ
PERSPICVÆ VTILITATIS ET
IVCVNDÆ MEDITATIONIS
MICHAELIS MEIERI.

FRANCOFVRTI,

Another important text from the *Musaeum Hermeticum* is the *Secreta Chymiae* by Michael Maier. The allegorical design portrays the lame man (the one who has no inner knowledge) and the initiate (the one possessed of the secret lore), both living in the same enchanted forest, which is the world.

The Key (*Clavis*) from *The Keys of Basil Valentine*, which was also reprinted in the *Musaeum Hermeticum*. It includes many of the standard hermetic symbols used by the alchemists and Rosicrucians.

who writes of the 'secret of the stone', from which the monk Basilius is supposed to have extracted a magical Quintessence which he used to cure people. This is generally supposed to symbolize the intention lying behind the practice of the secret hermetic art; that is, abstraction of the inner healing spirit from the material realm. Included also in the texts is the work of a man who may well have been a monk from the Benedictine abbey at Lammspring, near Hildesheim. Under the name of Lambsprinck, he wrote the hermetic *De Lapide Philosophico*, a work containing many curious alchemical figures of mythological creatures. The only English alchemical author of these texts is Thomas Norton, who informs us that he was rebuilding the church of St Mary Redcliffe in Bristol, probably with the aid of gold he had made by means of alchemical transmutation. Among the German Rosicrucian texts was the *Subtilis Allegoria* of Michael Maier, physician to the German Emperor. The title page of his treatise portrays the solar and lunar trees, the former being watered by the personification of old man Saturn.

Oppenheim was another centre of Rosicrucian publishing, though in modern times little of esoteric interest is preserved there. The original Rathaus (now partly a café) is still in existence, along with several beautiful medieval houses. Of particular interest to the occultist is the incised and gilded solar-lumar sundial with its planetary figures on the south wall of the Katherinenkirche, behind the Rathaus.

It was while he was travelling to Oxford, where he was to live in exile for some years, that Daniel Stolcius called on the publisher Luca Jennis, who showed him a large number of copperplate engravings which he had used over a number of years, most of them dealing with Rosicrucian and alchemical themes. Jennis suggested to the young Stolcius that he should write Latin verses interpreting some of the pictures, and publish them in a book. Accordingly, Stolcius took over 100 of the plates to construct around them short Latin poems, while living in Oxford. So it happened that in 1624 the *Viridarium Chymicum* was published in Frankfurt am Main, and immediately gained fame as the leading picture-encyclopaedia of contemporary alchemy. The two main sources of the plates were the alchemists Michael Maier and Daniel Mylius, whose books had been published by Jennis during the preceding decade. Several of the enigmatic plates depict the 12 states of Alchemy, and what Stolcius called the Champions of Alchemy (alchemists from what he termed the 'twelve nations'). Among them are Hermes Trismegistus of Egypt, Mary the Hebrew, Democritus the Greek, Morienes the Roman, Avicenna the Arab, Albertus Magnus the German, and so on.

A typical alchemical 'mystery' print, from Michael Maier's *Symbola Aurea Mensae* of 1617. The androgyne figure to the left is sometimes called the Rebis: it symbolizes the union of the Sun and Moon, of the male and female, or of those separate dualities upon which the ordinary perception of the world depends. The establishing of such a union is regarded as a necessary prelude to the successful alchemical operation. In its right hand, the androgyne holds the Pythagorean Y, which symbolizes the choice of a two-fold path. Only the person with the true grasp of the alchemical method will know which of the pathways to choose. The figure to the right is the great medieval scholar, Albertus Magnus, one of the 'Champions of Alchemy'.

This print from Daniel Stolcius's *Viridarium Chymicum* shows Mercury, with the traditional caduceus and winged feet, standing between representatives of the male Sun and the female Moon. It illustrates the alchemical operation called 'Separatio' – the separation of the female and male elements, or the separation of the light from the dross, which is one of the basic alchemical processes in the manufacture of the philosopher's stone.

Johann Daniel Mylius was from Wetterau in Hesse. Most of his occult works were published by Jennis, and plates from these works appear in a wide variety of alchemical texts. His most important selection of pictures was that contained in the influential *Philosophia Reformata*, written in 1620 at Frankfurt shortly after the defeat of Frederick V and Elizabeth of Bohemia (the Winter King and Queen), who were intimately connected with the spread of the Rosicrucian movement through Germany.

Heinrich Khunrath, another important figure, studied at the University of Basle, graduating from there in 1588. (A copy of his graduation thesis is in the British Library.) Afterwards he travelled widely in Germany to study esoteric matters, and in 1598, while in Bremen, met Dr John Dee. In his autobiography, Khunrath claimed to have discovered how to make the philosopher's stone – the aim of all true alchemists. In the writings and illustrations of Heinrich Khunrath we find a perfect mingling of the different streams which are now recognised as contributing to the growth of genuine Rosicrucian thought, that is esoteric mystical Christianity related to the ancient Mystery Wisdom, alchemical lore in its aspect of an inner science of the soul, and an insistence on reading the book of nature for a clue to the meaning of the world and life. Among the many beautiful plates from his *Amphitheatre of Eternal Wisdom* is the famous roundel showing the secret workshop of the Alchemist. In the text of this work, Khunrath provides 365 esoteric meditations, one for each day of the year.

Daniel Cramer was a Protestant theologian who lectured at the Academies of Stetten and Wittenberg. He produced a most important collection of 40 emblematic hieroglyphics with short Latin commentaries, which was published at Frankfurt in 1617. The emblems contained in this book are quite openly symbolic of the Rosy-Cross, though the overt symbolism is actually concerned with the various forms of the human heart. The modern historian Adam McLean has drawn a connection here with the Tantric tradition of meditations linked to the *chakra*s, those invisible soul-centres in the human spiritual body which occultists liken to rapidly-moving wheels of fire. More work has to be done comparing what is known of Rosicrucianism with Tantra, a cult pre-dating Hinduism which has suffered continual repression over the centuries. Some of the similarities are striking. Both systems involve arduous preparation and discipline: an adept must strive to understand highly sophisticated concepts which are often cloaked in elaborate symbolism and allusion. The ultimate aim of both Tantra and Rosicrucianism is the release and control of the almost limitless spiritual energy contained within each individual, for which the body is simply a vehicle.

Baptista Van Helmont (left) and his son, Franciscus. Baptista's ear is placed over his son's eye to indicate that he had initiated his son into the hermetic art. English Rosicrucianism owes much to Franciscus Van Helmont.

THE MYSTERIOUS CIRCLE AT RAGLEY

Few esoteric centres in Europe can have been as influential on the history of a country as was Ragley in Warwickshire during the late seventeenth and early eighteenth centuries. During this period, Ragley was established as the centre for the study of Rosicrucianism in England, under the patronage of Anne Finch, Viscountess Conway. It was here that many of the great men of the time gathered to discuss the secrets of the 'Fraternity', as the followers of the Rosy-Cross were called, and to pursue a diverse programme of studies related to occult, esoteric, cabbalistic and related fields of thought.

The practical teachings and knowledge of the Fraternity appear to have been introduced to Lady Conway – and thence to Ragley – by Franciscus Van Helmont, one of the more unconventional members of the brotherhood.

It is likely that Lady Conway's tutor, Henry More, introduced Van Helmont to Ezechiel Foxcroft in 1670 at his rooms in Cambridge, where he was a lecturer in mathematics at King's College. Certainly the two great men met on that occasion, for it is recorded that Foxcroft was able to understand Van Helmont's native Dutch – even though Van Helmont was prepared to speak with equal facility in French or Italian. It was probably as a result of this Cambridge meeting that Van Helmont introduced Foxcroft to that most remarkable of all Rosicrucian texts, *The Chymical Wedding*, which the Cambridge scholar soon translated into English. He also introduced More to the work of Baron Von Rosenroth's (another member of the Ragley circle) on the Jewish *Zohar*. Perhaps it was Henry More who introduced Van Helmont to Lady Conway, for within a short time of the Cambridge meeting he was established at Ragley, nominally as her physician, but actually as her tutor in alchemical, Rosicrucian and mystical subjects.

In fact, Lady Conway was no stranger to the theory of occult and mystical lore, for before she met Van Helmont she had read, among other esoteric works, the books of the influential German occultist, mystic (and incidentally, Rosicrucian), Jacob Boehme. Probably, however, Van Helmont was the first Rosicrucian she met who recognised the importance of Ragley as a centre for the propagation of such esoteric ideas, and who undertook to instruct her in the spiritual disciplines and knowledge attached to the secret art.

The most famous portrait of Van Helmont, now in the Tate Gallery but formerly hung at Ragley, was painted by Sir Peter Lely, in England, possibly for Lady Conway. Few could guess from this sophisticated and polished exterior the extent of his nonconformity, or the source of his urbane wisdom. Van Helmont had spent the early years of his life travelling through Europe among a group of wandering gypsies, mainly in order to study their language and customs. Although he was without doubt a Rosicrucian (and therefore involved with the study of the inner secrets of Man and the universe, rather than with the attainment of 'outer wealth'), he gained notoriety among ordinary men as a successful alchemist. He was thought to have discovered the secrets of making gold, and it was widely believed that he manufactured his considerable riches in his alchemical laboratories.

It was his decision to follow the gentlemen of the road, and learn their secret lore, which gave Van Helmont an unlooked-for place in English literature, for his story was adopted by the Victorian poet Matthew Arnold who made him the hero for his poem *The Scholar Gypsy* (1853):

> And grave Glanvil did the tale inscribe
> That thou wert wander'd from the studious walls
> To learn strange arts, and join a gipsy-tribe

Arnold read about Van Helmont in a description left by one of the Ragley group, Joseph Glanvill, whose activities we shall examine shortly. According to Arnold's own notes, he had the story from Glanvill's *Vanity of Dogmatizing* (1661), which places the scholar-gipsy as a former student of Oxford, forced into the company of vagabonds by poverty, who later insisted that when he had compassed the whole secret of their art, he would 'give the world an account of what he had learned'. The gipsies with whom Van Helmont lived were 'Bohemians', and, as we have seen, the Rosicrucian movement had flourished for a brief time in Bohemia; so we may take it that Glanvill, in mentioning his own university as the origin for the scholar-gipsy was merely disguising the well-known story of his companion Van Helmont.

Far from being an elegiac poem, Arnold's *The Scholar Gipsy* is really an esoteric one. The poet imagines that he has caught a glimpse of the erstwhile Oxford scholar in the countryside near the city, 200 years after Glanvill had told the tale, and an equal period after the supposed death of the scholar. Arnold imagines that he did not die like ordinary men, for he had not been worn out by the 'repeated shocks' of ordinary life:

> But thou possessest an immortal lot,
> And we imagine thee exempt from age.

The notion of an undying scholar-gipsy has not come from the pen of Glanvill, yet may well be derived from the writings of Van Helmont himself. The Rosicrucian had been a proponent of a strange theory of reincarnation, which truly gives Man exemption from age. The result of this belief – no doubt derived from his Rosicrucian studies – is the earliest non-classical account of reincarnation theory to be expressed in the English language, and is argued from Scripture.

The theory put forward by Van Helmont does not correspond in every detail to that held by modern occultists, for he maintained that everyone has 12 repeated earth-lives or, as he called them, 'Revolutions'. The Rosicrucians and occultists of that period were accustomed to disguising their words with what are called blinds, however, and it may be that Van Helmont was referring to a notion that a human spirit dwells alternately in a male and female body once in every zodiacal period. Thus, for example, while the Sun is precessing through the zodiacal sign Pisces, the human spirit would incarnate once in female form and once in male form to experience the conditions of that 'zodiacal age'. It would then reincarnate in male and female form in the next great age as

Two engravings from an eighteenth-century book by Georg Welling. The one to the left shows the outpouring of the eternal triad, its subsequent separation into dualities, and the passage of the cosmic power through the spheres. The engraving to the right is the earliest-known western diagram representing a theory of reincarnation, in which each human spirit is born again twice (in male and female bodies) in every zodiacal age.

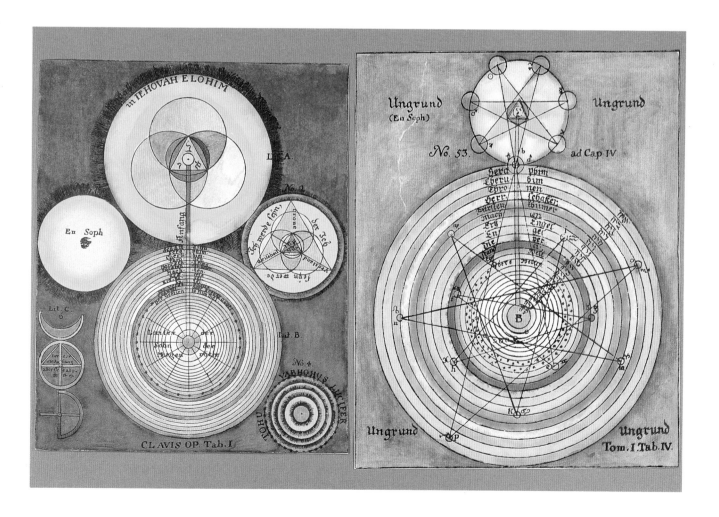

the Sun fell back (by precession) into Aquarius. The notion of 'twelve incarnations' or revolutions, therefore, may be a way in which the alchemist introduced this notion of reincarnation in an age totally unequipped to accept such a belief. Some idea of the 'twelve revolutions' or rebirths is hinted at in one of the plates in George Welling's *Opus Mago-Cabbalisticum et Theosophicum* (1784 edition).

Van Helmont, no doubt acting in his capacity as family doctor, was present when Lady Conway died at Ragley, and since her husband was absent on business he had a special coffin made to contain the body. The coffin was of a double form, with the inner part made from glass and the outer from wood. Her body was placed in the glass coffin, immersed in a special liquid, the formula of which Van Helmont was said to have learned from his father, who had also been a Rosicrucian. This strange structure permitted Lady Conway's husband to view the preserved body before burial, the double-coffin later being encased in an outer covering of lead at nearby Arrow church. This coffin is still preserved in Arrow church, near Ragley.

Lady Conway's only written work was originally in Latin. This was taken by Van Helmont to Amsterdam shortly after her death, and translated into English for publication in London in 1692 as *The Principles of the Most Ancient and Modern Philosophy*.

Who was this 'grave Glanvil' whose name survived in a nineteenth-century poem on the scholar gipsy? Was he also connected with the curious circle at Ragley? Indeed he was — and perhaps it was due to this that Ragley itself gained such notoriety for the gatherings of wise men which took place within its walls and gardens; particularly those in which was evinced an interest in the supernatural. There is some indication that elementary spirit-raising (what we would nowadays call seances) was conducted at Ragley, perhaps at the request of the Joseph Glanvill who often joined the groups in their discussions. Joseph Glanvill, at one time chaplain to King Charles II and a Fellow of the Royal Society, had become interested in the occult through strange stories about the Tedworth Drummer, which he sought to explain in scientific terms.

The Tedworth Drummer was a case of what was perhaps poltegeist activity, beginning in April 1662 and lasting for about a year. It involved strange drumming sounds issuing from around the house of the magistrate John Mompesson in Tedworth (now Tidsworth) in Hampshire, along with other unaccountable psychic phenomena. Glanvill went to Tedworth to investigate at first hand the phenomenon, and to take the statements of witnesses. He was therefore one of the first people to attempt an objective assessment of psychic phenomena. When, later, Charles II sent a special committee to report on the famous hauntings, they found nothing, though the majority of those investigating were (like Glanvill) convinced of the psychic origin of the manifestations.

Glanvill's interest soon led him to a firm belief that psychic phenomena, and related witchcraft, should be examined in a new light. He was one of the first Englishmen to write in opposition to the popular view of witchcraft, at a time when witches were being hanged in great numbers throughout the land. His *Saducismus Triumphatus, or full and plain evidence concerning witches and apparitions* contained a frontispiece that represented six of the most famous 'well attested' cases of witchcraft and psychic phenomena. The book was a great success, and contributed largely to growth of the belief that witchcraft belonged in the realm of superstition, and should be studied more objectively. An image on the frontispiece shows the Tedworth Drummer in the very material form of a winged demon, surrounded by its minions (the demon drummer was never actually seen, merely heard). Another image is a celestial apparition at Amsterdam — a story which he probably had from Van Helmont himself.

In his writings, Glanvill did not deny the reality of witchcraft but claimed that the majority of men and women accused of the crime were not guilty and probably suffered from delusions. He also made the very valid point that belief of witchcraft was almost atheistic in that it apportioned greater power to the Devil than to God. Most of all, he argued that witchcraft — and indeed, the whole realm of the supernatural — should be subjected to a thorough intellectual survey with a view to understanding its nature. Glanvill is now regarded as 'the father of modern psychical research'; though it is clear that he could not pull himself free from the prejudices of his age, showing levels of credulity which would not pass muster in our own time.

The Tedworth Drummer, shown here as a demon beating a drum and surrounded by demonic serpents. An illustration from Joseph Glanvill's *Saducismus Triumphatus*, 1683.

It is likely that not all those who met at Ragley were Rosicrucians, though many of them were. Among the members of this loose-knit group surrounding Lady Conway were the philosopher Dr Henry More (her tutor), who wrote so forcefully against the influential materialism of Descartes and Hobbes, Elizabeth Foxcroft, the mother of Ezechiel Foxcroft, the translator of the early Rosicrucian text *The Chymical Wedding*, the Cambridge Platonist and scholar Ralph Cudworth, Valentine Greatrakes, the Irish healer who cured thousands of people of a variety of illnesses merely by means of his touch, and many others.

Among these, perhaps the most influential was Robert Boyle (1627–1691), chemist, philosopher, scientist and alchemist, founding member of the Royal Society, and undoubtedly a Rosicrucian. Just as Foxcroft had introduced the ideas of the secret fraternity to Cambridge, so Boyle introduced them to receptive minds in Oxford. In 1659 he invited to this city the Rosicrucian Peter Sthael, who had formerly been established in Strasbourg. The nominal idea was that Sthael was to tutor Boyle in geometry, philosophy and chemistry. The circle he tutored was in no need of such instruction, however, for it included Christopher Wren, already a brilliant geometer and architect, John Locke, perhaps the most important English intellectual of his day; and many others who afterwards influenced the course of history.

In his *Sceptical Chymist* (1661), Boyle had been critical of the theory that the world of matter was composed of either the occult 'Four Elements' (Earth, Air, Fire and Water) or of the alchemical 'Three Principles' (Salt, Mercury and Sulphur), and introduced instead the definition of the chemical elements which is accepted to this day. He was therefore one of the seminal forces which opened the world of science to modern materialistic thought, for the occult and alchemical view of the Four Elements and the Three Principles had been rooted in a spiritual view of the cosmos. (Such a view, had it persisted, would have impeded the growth of the materialistic outlook which would be necessary in the centuries to come if Man was to understand in a new way the real

A detail of the gigantic Atomium in Brussels, which some occultists have compared to both the spiritual web which maintains the nature of matter, and to the Cabbalistic tree of the Sephiroth, one of the most important of all occult diagrams.

An early (nineteenth century) drawing of the atom based on clairvoyant vision, published for the first time in Edwin Babbitt's *Principles of Light and Color*, 1878, a book which had a profound influence on the development of occult art.

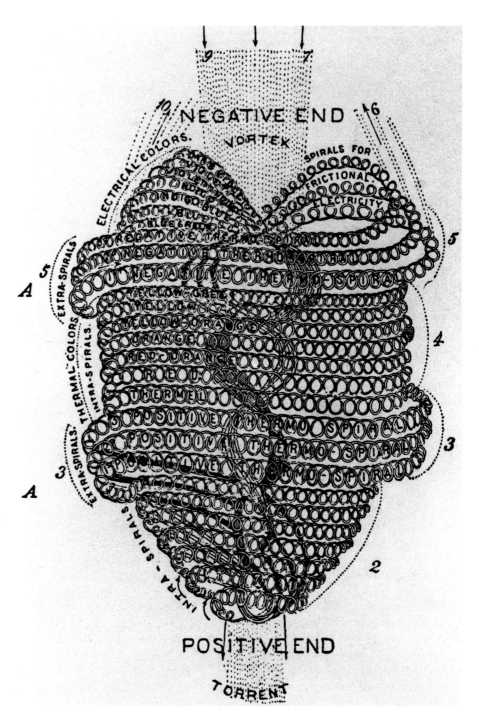

structure of matter.) The modern atomic theory has been ascribed to Boyle, though it was left to Lavoisier, in the next century, to draw up the first list of identified elements. Boyle, who was widely read in occult matters, would have known that the alchemists did not teach the theory of the four elements, as is popularly believed, like other esotericists, he held that there were five elements, the four elements (Earth, Air, Fire and Water) being united within the formative force of a fifth element, or Quintessence.

It is perhaps an aside to point out that the gigantic Atomium in Brussels is almost as much a memorial to occult lore as it is to modern scientific achievement. Not only was the molecular theory announced by men who were essentially alchemists, but the earliest drawing of an atom appeared in a work of an occult nature, Edwin Babbitt's *Principles of Light and Color*, published in the United States in 1878. Furthermore, the schematic representation of the atom in Brussels closely resembles that fundamental occult diagram, the Sephirothic tree of the Cabbalists.

Specialists in occult symbolism point out that the many fascinating plates in George Welling's remarkable Rosicrucian work, *Opus Mago-Cabbalisticum et Theoso-phicum* (1784) are based on the teachings of Van Helmont. Many of these, similar in some respects to the plates used to illustrate the William Law edition of Jacob Boehme, are esoteric parables about the relationship between the cosmos and Man. In the book, cabbalistic terms (such as 'En Soph' and 'Jehovah Elohim') mingle with German Christian terms, indicating that the work is of that order recognised as 'Christian cabbalism' – the syncretic merging of the secret Jewish tradition with esoteric Christian lore. The triple-crescented sigil to the lower left of the design marks the beginning of all creation, and is itself a summary of Rosicrucian lore being based on the sigil originated by John Dee. The large lower circle portrays the nine hierarchies of the Christian lore (linked with the planetary spheres) in a most unconventional inversion (the stars below the sphere of earth and with the realm of Lucifer at the centre of creation). The sun symbol at the centre of this circle is directly linked with the sun symbol of the upper circle, centred on a triad of circles (the Holy Trinity, but also the Three Principles of the alchemists: Salt, Mercury and Sulphur).

ROSICRUCIANS AND THE ANCIENT TRADITION

The Rosicrucian movement which was developed in English society on the estates of Lady Conway at Ragley was deeply concerned with merging all that was of spiritual importance in the Christian stream of thought with the ancient traditions of esotericism and occultism. The most influential of the early Rosicrucian texts, *The Chymical Wedding* had been written before 1616, but was first printed in Strasbourg in that year. Two earlier texts, dealing with this strange esoteric group or Fraternity, were *The Fama*, which appeared in Kassel, in 1614, and the *Confession* the following year. It does seem, however, that the manuscripts of all three titles were circulated for at least a decade before this time. Some modern historians believe that the castle to which Christian Rosencreutz is led in *The Chymical Wedding* had an actual existence in the Bohemian castle of Karlstejn, a few miles from Prague, although, as we have seen, at least one modern scholar has suggested that the castle at Heidelberg was the original site.

One thing is certain, however: the chain of Rosicrucian ideas may be traced, in changing form, right into our own century. Indeed, the modern occultist Rudolf Steiner, who was one of the most brilliant in a long line of Rosicrucians, saw a chain of influence between the early Rosicrucian literature; the secret diagrams of Henricus Madathanus Theosophus in *Die Geheimen Figuren der Rosenkreuzer*, published in Altona in 1785; and the writings of that strange occult genius, H. P. Blavatsky – especially in her *Isis Unveiled*.

The wide publicity which the hidden fellowship of Rosicrucians attained during the 17th and 18th century tends to overshadow many of the other important esoteric groups which existed in Europe during that time. These included several offshoots from the Rosicrucian movement, yet the most important fraternity was that which (rightly or wrongly) claimed origins in the secret bodies which had governed the mystery of the cathedral builders during the late Middle Ages. These alchemical and masonic groups were both numerous and politically influential in all European countries until well into the nineteenth century.

In France, the cities of Paris, Lyons and La Rochelle were important alchemical centres. The cathedrals of Notre-Dame in Paris and Amiens have on their façades a whole series of images which relate to the astrological and alchemical keys of hermetic science. Denis Zachaire, an alchemist of the sixteenth century, has left a detailed account of how:

> Not a day passed, even on feast-days and Sundays, without our gathering together either at the lodging of a member of our group, or at the great Notre Dame, which is the church of most resort in Paris, to debate the tasks of the day preceding.

Esotericists such as Fulcanelli, who has revealed many of the hermetic designs of the façades of French cathedrals, lament the fact that the majority of nineteenth-century

A group of 'gargoyles', which are
in fact symbolic figures rooted in
alchemical lore, on the façade of
the tower of Notre-Dame in Paris.
The Pelican is a name given to one
of the stages in the alchemical
process: it is also a symbol of
Christ, and a most important
Rosicrucian symbol.

On the façade of Notre-Dame, in
Paris, there are a group of relief
figures each bearing roundels on
which are symbolized the various
stages in the 'Great Work' of
alchemy. Note the resemblance
between the single snake curling
around an upright rod, and the
entwined snakes in the caduceus of
the Stolcius print on page 137.

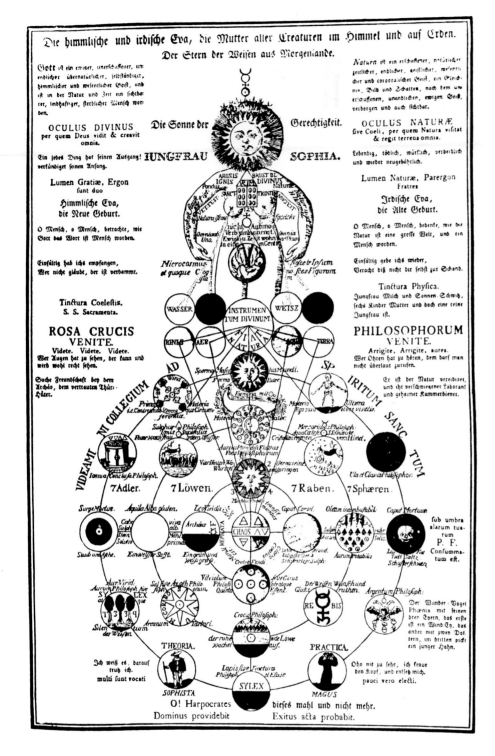

One of the intriguing Rosicrucian-alchemical texts published at Altona in 1785 in *Die Lehren der Rosenkreuzer . . .* The diagram combines many elements from a variety of occult systems, such as the Gnostic image of the fall of Sophia, and the child (in the womb) born from this fall, which is the World itself. The fall, or birth, of this child symbolizes the descent into the four-fold elements of Earth, Air, Fire and Water, which are maintained in equilibrium by the Quintessence. The symbols for the elements are below the 'Jungfrau Sophia', but are also at the very centre of the concentrics, which mark the seven heavenly or planetary spheres. The circles centred on the outer concentric do not represent the twelve zodiacal arcs, as one might expect, but the twelve stages in the alchemical operation.

restorations have resulted in an alteration of the hermetic symbols which once covered the surfaces of the great cathedrals. Even so, many of the alchemical hieroglyphics have survived. Details on the shields or roundels in the hands of figures on the central porch of Notre Dame depict such alchemical items as the mystical athenor, the Philosopher's Stone, the Four Elements, and symbols which reveal the various admixtures or conjunctions of the secret recipes for Sulphur, Salt and Mercury.

One of the most remarkable yet enigmatic of all alchemo-Rosicrucian texts is the *Book Without Words* (in Latin, *Mutus Liber*), printed in 1677 for Jacob Saulat in La Rochelle, which city appears to have been an important alchemical centre in the seventeenth century. The name given for this author (properly speaking, in a wordless book, the designation should be designer) is Altus, which, besides meaning highest in

The Star card from a nineteenth-century Italian Tarot pack. Some occultists link the imagery of this card with the opera *The Magic Flute*, which features the Star-Flaming Queen.

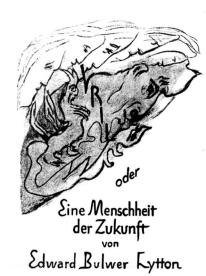

An interesting jacket design for the book *Vril*, by Edward Bulwer Lytton, which popularized the notion of the terrible sidereal force vril, already recognised in Rosicrucian circles as a secret power possessed by the Atlanteans.

Latin – and therefore standing as a reference to a high degree of initiation – is also a play on the name Saulet. As the title implies, the book consists of a series of enigmatic plates relating to both alchemical and Rosicrucian symbolism. Only the title page, or opening illustration, contains a number of words in Latin; these may be translated as 'The Wordless Book, in which nevertheless all the secret philosophy is revealed in hieroglyphic figures, consecrated to the thrice blessed, merciful and greatest God, dedicated only to the sons of the art (that is, the art of alchemy), the name of the author being Altus'. There follows a number of obscure figures, in the form of what may be bibliographic references, but these have never been adequately explained. The importance of the book may be seen in the fact that Altus sought protection for his copyright from the King of France.

Besides its undoubted importance as a Rosicrucian centre, France was also an influential masonic centre, and it is recorded that up to the time of the French Revolution, there were well over 500 different lodges throughout the kingdom. The situation was very much the same in Germany and Austria, for the masonic fraternity played an important part in the regeneration of the arts, sciences and social life in those countries. For some years, Mozart's opera *The Magic Flute* has been recognised as containing symbols and ideas directly linked to a stream of hermetic symbolism, yet it is only comparatively recently that the musicologist, Jacques Chailley, has researched the subject fully and brought together all the different strands of masonic and occult symbolism within the work. One of the masonic secrets revealed in the libretto's transformation symbolism is the curious golden padlock. This is used by the Three Ladies to lock the mouth of the bird-catcher, Papageno, as a punishment for having told a lie. As Chailley points out, the heart-shape of the padlock recalls the shape of the symbolic golden trowel used in the Lodge of Adoption's rituals for sealing the postulant's mouth. In fact, the heart itself was often used in occult symbolism to relate to the hidden ('unspoken') parts of man which we have already glanced at in images used by the Rosicrucian Cramer.

Not only are many of the symbols and rituals within Mozart's opera derived directly from masonic symbolism, but even some of his terminology belongs to the hermetic tradition. A fine example is the flaming star which is one of the symbols depicted on the masonic apron, and which is figured in the opera in the name of the Star-Flaming Queen. This particular masonic symbol is expressed in the Tarot card as The Star, which depicts a naked woman pouring water to the earth, and which has been associated with zodiacal Aquarius, Mozart's own horoscope sign. The grotto at Aigen, north of Salzburg, where Mozart was born and lived for some years, has a decorated temple portal, and a nearby cascade, both of which have long been associated with the occult sects of the Illuminati and the Masons. The symbolism of water plays an important part in the opera – for example, the 'baptism by water' which occurs when the bird-catcher throws water over the face of his future wife. It has been suggested that Mozart may have been present at meetings held within the grotto itself.

There is a legend that Mozart was poisoned with mercury by his brother masons for having disclosed some of their deeper secrets in the remarkable *Magic Flute*. However, there is no truth in this story, and indeed the evidence suggests that several practising masons actually helped in the writing of the libretto and in the production of the opera itself.

The novelist, Edward Bulwer Lytton, who wrote a large number of romances linked with the occult tradition, was a member of the nineteenth-century Rosicrucian group, the Societas Rosicruciana Anglia. Bulwer Lytton lived at Knebworth House in Hertfordshire, and it was here that Douglas Home, the clairvoyant, witnessed the novelist, in a seance, make contact with a spirit which claimed to have influenced the author in his writing of the romance *Zanoni*. Another novel, *The Coming Race*, had a more sinister effect on world history than even Bulwer Lytton would have been happy with, for certain of the ideas relating to the Utopian master race of this text – a race possessing the extraordinary destructive power of Vril – certainly influenced the black-magical ideas adopted by the Nazi party in the late '20s and '30s of our century. The Vril Society, which was founded in Berlin prior to World War II, was based on Bulwer Lytton's romantic vision, expressed in the words of Blavatsky in *The Secret Doctrine*.

Vril is '. . . the terrible sidereal Force, known to, and named by the Atlanteans Mash-Mak, and by the Aryan Rishis in their 'Ashtar Vidya' by a name that we do not like to give. It is the vril of Bulwer Lytton's *Coming Race*, and of the coming races of our mankind. The name vril may be a fiction; the Force itself is a fact doubted as little in India as the existence of their Rishis, since it is mentioned in all their secret works. It is this vibratory Force, which . . . reduces to ashes 100,000 men and elephants, as easily as it would a dead rat . . . And it is this Satanic Force that our generations were to be allowed to add to their stock of Anarchist's baby-toys . . . It is this destructive agency, which, once in the hands of some modern Attila . . . would reduce Europe in a few days to its primitive chaotic state with no man left alive to tell the tale.

THE SURVIVAL OF THE ROSICRUCIANS

The Rosicrucian stream of thought did not die out after the great flowering of the seventeenth century – indeed, it is relatively easy to trace the gradual transformation of its tenets into certain modern esoteric movements, such as Anthroposophy. Many modern artists, such as Mondrian and Kandinsky, have been influenced by the development of Rosicrucian ideas, in the first case through the writings of Blavatsky, and in the second by the lectures of Steiner.

Less well known, however, is the influence of esoteric thought on Antoni Gaudí, the creator of what the artist Salvador Dali called 'edible architecture'. Gaudí began his masterpiece, the church of Sagrada Familia in Barcelona, in 1884. Work on the structure has continued ever since, and it is calculated that it will not be completed for another hundred years. From a strictly architectural point of view, it is probably the most remarkable church ever to have been conceived, yet it contains within it symbolic evidence of Gaudí's interest in occult and Rosicrucian thought. Even the 'icing sugar' finials on the top of the Sagrada's four towers reflect an esoteric tradition, for the numbers of the small balls represent (numerologically) a spiritual energy which is carried skywards by the four towers. If we visualise the four towers as representing the four elements of Earth, Air, Fire and Water (bearing upwards a spiritual charge of power which is the magical Quintessence) and if we note that the spires are linked together in pairs, reflecting the 'harmony' between Fire-Air and Water-Earth, we may begin to sense just how daring is Gaudí's conception.

It is likely that for some time Gaudí fell under the influence of the occultist Joséphin Péladan, who headed the influential Cabbalistic Order of the Rosy Cross, allegedly rooted in Rosicrucian teachings. In fact Péladan had a considerable influence on several artists and writers including Gauguin, Mallarmé and Verlaine, as well as the composer Erik Satie. Péladan proposed the notion that art was not properly conditioned by materialistic elements, and should strive to express the inexpressible, the indefinable, the aspirational, rather than aspects of the material realm. This view of Art is perhaps supremely expressed in Sagrada Familia. The small church of Rennes-le-Château in southern France has also become a centre of occult pilgrimage in modern times. Its interior was designed by another individual who fell under the influence of Péladan – Beringer Saunière – who is responsible for many other buildings, such as the small library-château and a house. In pointing to the influence of Péladan on the early twentieth century, however, we should observe that his version of Rosicrucianism was very different to that proposed in seventeenth-century literature.

Although the traditional forms of alchemy have been largely swamped by scientific methods, and are now in the hands of only a small group of dedicated individuals, masonry and Rosicrucianism still flourish in Europe in a variety of different forms. The number of different groups claiming connection with such arcane streams as masonry, Rosicrucianism, Templar wisdom – or through the received teachings of such remarkable individuals as Blavatsky, Steiner, Gurdjieff, and so on – is almost confusing, yet the fact is that the old concept of 'hidden fraternities' (groups of men or women working in exclusive secrecy) is now less insistent. The more wholesome arcane societies and groups usually publish literature which sets out their aims, their occult aspirations, and their various credos.

Pen and ink portrait of the great esotericist Rudolf Steiner.

Detail of the towers of the Sagrada
Familia in Barcelona, which was
begun by Antoni Gaudí in 1884,
and still remains unfinished.

In modern times the most remarkable of all centres for the study and dissemination
of esoteric knowledge is the magnificent concrete palace-fortress of the Goetheanum at
Dornach, in Switzerland, built as a centre for the Anthroposophical movement
according to the design of Rudolf Steiner. The foundations of this building were laid,
according to the ancient principles of orientation, with symbolic corner-stones; the
moment of inception being 6.30 p.m. local time on 20 September 1913, when Mercury
stood in Libra. The foundation stone itself, placed directly beneath the point where the
speakers desk would be within the main hall, consisted of two interpenetrating
pentagondodecahedrons, formed from copper, orientated towards specific points.

According to Steiner, the 'stone' represented the striving human soul immersed as a microcosm within the macrocosm.

The first Goetheanum, constructed of wood, was burned down by a vandal whom some have linked with the Nazi party, on New Year's Eve, 1922–23. Steiner regarded the original foundation stone as appropriate to form the same function for a new building, which he designed and constructed on entirely new architectural principles. In the entire history of European architecture, there has been nothing quite like the Goetheanum. It seems to be an organic outflowing from the Jura landscape in which it was built. Steiner designed it in such a way that its outer form would reflect absolutely its inner use and purpose – its design was intended to express that form which arises in human perceptions and feelings when the soul receives the living essence of modern Rosicrucian teachings. With such thoughts in mind, the Goetheanum could not fail to be an earthly expression of the science of spirit, its outer form expressive of inner hidden laws. In Steiner's view, true symbols were not static things but spiritual forms in metamorphosis. His own remarkable work was expressive of this almost Goetheian view of art, linked with a healthy clairvoyance which could perceive the forms of the spiritual world, vision of which is normally denied to Man.

The Goetheanum is still used as a centre for living arts, such as drama, painting and eurythmics – that remarkable form of movement which the uninitiated associate with dance – and with the study of speech and music. Anyone who is interested in esoteric ideas cannot afford not to visit the Goetheanum. An interesting final point is that Steiner claimed that the ruined castle on the hill above his Goetheanum was one of the Grail castles, linked with the hermetic esoteric Christian tradition.

6 Stones and Magic Symbols

The circle of stones at Callanish on the island of Lewis, Scotland. Many occultists claim that these stone circles, which were certainly designed as solar-lunar calendars, were constructed by men with a superior level of awareness of cosmic realities.

Overleaf: the prehistoric alignment at Kermario, to the north-east of Carnac, in France. It has been dated to about 2,400 BC.

THE earliest historical records point to a Europe geographically different from our modern landmasses, occupied by a race called the Iberians. Occult historians, writing of a period as early as 5,000 BC, refer to these people as the Sicanes, but the Greek historian Strabo calls them the Turduli. Strabo notes that these ancient peoples had their own language and writing, along with a set of epic poems and laws for which they claimed an antiquity of over 6,000 years, implying that these people were the cultural leaders in Europe circa 10,000 BC. The historian of the lost continent of Atlantis, Ignatius Donnelly, had no hesitation in linking this race with the survivors of the final deluge which removed almost all traces of their civilization, nor in claiming that descendants of the European Iberians are to be found among modern Basques.

The literature of occultism is filled with references to the continent of Atlantis, and several maps have been made in order to show its former extent in relation to the modern continents of Europe, Africa and the Americas. One of the earliest of such maps is that reproduced by the polymath esotericist Athanasius Kircher, who based his findings mainly on classical literature. Later maps, almost certainly constructed on information obtained by clairvoyant means, more or less confirm the location of the continent, plumb in the middle of the modern Atlantic ocean, yet redefine its contours and site with greater precision the locations of its main cities. According to the accounts preserved in esoteric literature, Atlantis did not sink beneath the Atlantic in one single inundation; the inundation, though dramatic enough and certainly, at times on a cataclysmic scale, took place over a period of many centuries. It is only the final sinking of the last remnants of the old continent, in the form of two islands called Ruta and Daitya, that Plato records as a single island in his own survey of the Atlantean myth.

Not all traces of Atlantis have been lost, however. Remains of the ancient culture, which involved the use of fantastic powers over natural forces (powers which have long been lost to mankind), as well as a deep knowledge of the secrets behind the forms of nature, and a polytheistic religion expressed in pyramid buildings and a cosmic cult are still found in the ancient Mayan and Aztec sites of South America. The survival of Atlantean culture in Europe is of a different order, for it appears to have been the work of less sophisticated survivors of the once vast civilization, the peoples of which perished with the sinking of the continent or dispersed into Asia in vast migrations. Esotericists who concern themselves with such matters claim that in parts of France, Spain, England and Scotland there exist many remains of the Iberian culture which, at the beginning of our history, still clung to the Atlantean rites and customs. Among these are the vast cosmic temples of Callanish on the remote island of Lewis, the most famous of all such circles at Stonehenge, and the vast megaliths at Carnac in France. The occultist Blavatsky, who has provided many remarkable insights into the builders of these stones and their remaining structures, claims that these stone circles, like many of the logan stones and the so-called 'speaking stones' which were once found in many parts of Europe, 'are the relics of the last Atlanteans'.

THE MYSTERY OF STONEHENGE

There are many ancient mysteries on Salisbury Plain, yet news of the unique mystery of Stonehenge appears to have reached the centre of the world even in ancient times, when Britain was a cartographic speck at the furthest-flung point of an empire, the despair of Roman soldiers anxious to return to a more equable clime. In the first century BC, the historian Diodorus Siculus, assiduously compiling his 40 books of world history, mentions that in northern Europe – 'in the land of the Hyperboreans' – there was an island wherein a spherical temple had been built. He remarks, almost in passing, that this temple was visited by the god Apollo every 19 years. There was nothing extraordinary to the Roman mind in the idea of a god visiting a temple – indeed, it was an essential part of the ancients' belief that a god would at times reside within the temple dedicated to him. It was even the practice for architects to incorporate inside their temples a special inner chamber to provide a sacred dwelling place for the god to whom the temple was dedicated. What is interesting about this early account, however, is that the temple mentioned by Diodorus was 'spherical' – a word which might reasonably be taken as referring to a circular ground plan.

An assumption has been made that the 'island' to which Diodorus refers is Britain, and that the 'spherical temple' is Stonehenge. However, it must be admitted that there are many other British circular-plan stone structures which might have been known to the Roman world – perhaps even the impressive circle at Castlerigg in Cumbria, or the huge complex of circles and earthworks at Avebury, to the north of Stonehenge. Whatever the specific circle Diodorus had in mind, we are still left with the question of what any of these stone circles had to do with a periodicity of 19 years, or even with the sun-god Apollo.

The ancient Romans knew of one cycle which corresponds very closely to the 19-year periodicity, but this does not relate only to the Sun for it measures a period-return of the Moon's node to a solar point. The movement of the nodes of the Moon is a gradual circling of the ecliptic (which of course marks the movement of the Sun) in a contrary direction to the planets. This 'lunar node cycle' is 18 years and seven months. In three of these nodal revolutions, which take a sequence of 56 years, the Moon completes a circuit of eclipses and then begins the same sequence again. The cycle describes a complete relationship between Sun and Moon. Is it possible that what the arrangement of uprights at Stonehenge marked was the periodicity of 18 years and seven months, which Diodorus Siculus then rounded up to 19 years?

Some authors – most notably Professor Gerald Hawkins of Boston University who followed outline-plans drawn up by earlier investigators – have treated the arrangement of stones as though it were a complex graphic computer of critical solar and lunar positions. In his *Stonehenge Decoded* Hawkins claims that ten of the alignments of the circle point to significant positions of the Sun, with an accuracy of under one degree;

while a different set of 14 alignments points to extreme positions of the Moon. Further, he notes that when the winter Moon rises over the horizon above the Heel Stone, then an eclipse of Sun or Moon will follow. The eclipse of Sun or Moon is one of the most obvious pointers to the 19-year cycle of Diodorus Siculus, for the lunar node is actually the point where the path of the Moon crosses the path of the Sun (the ecliptic).

Hawkins' own conclusions have been subjected to a battery of criticism, yet there may be little doubt that in some mysterious way the circle of stones *was* designed (perhaps among other things) to mark out significant solar-lunar positions, the most important of which was linked with the '19-year' cycle.

The importance of the nodal points in ancient times has not yet been fully appreciated by modern science, for it is directly related to the long-discarded occult view of the cosmos. In ancient times it was believed that when there was an eclipse of the Sun or the Moon, the short period marked a most suitable time for Mankind to

Sunset at Stonehenge, the most famous of the British stone circles, of which over five hundred are known to have survived.

commune with spirits. Whether these 'spirits' were demons or daemons would presumably be the concern of the magicians; the black magicians being concerned with making their pacts or requests to the darker demons; the white magicians, or initiates, being concerned with invoking the aid of angels, or even higher hierarchies. When Diodorus Siculus writes of 'Apollo' descending to the spherical temple, it is clear that he had in mind a visitation from a very high being indeed.

Whatever the validity of the ancient view of eclipses, we can at least understand why it was so important for the men of old to establish some method of predicting when they would occur. If the time of an eclipse were known, then it would be possible for the priests to prepare themselves and their community to receive the benefits bestowed from the spiritual world. They could also prepare effective counter-magic against the evil-working of the black magicians who might use the same periodicities for nefarious purposes.

The stone circle at Castlerigg. It is set on a plateau and surrounded by hills and mountains, which appear to play an important part in the measurement of solar and lunar orientations, and rising and setting patterns.

Two of the distinctive standing stones at Avebury, which in prehistoric times was the most extensive, and perhaps the most important, of all religious sites in Britain.

Stonehenge was a centre used for determining the most propitious moment to make contact with the higher spiritual beings, whom (it was then believed) were the fount of all human life and prosperity. Although Hawkins has been criticised on both stylistic and mathematical grounds, it is hard to doubt his general contention that certain stones, when viewed from fixed points, are designed to point to important solar and lunar positions. (The midsummer sunrise as it touches the top of the Heel Stone has become one of the most sought after images for photographers.) Hawkins points out that in 1800 BC the first flash of the sun would appear about three-quarters of a degree to the north (left), and a six-foot man standing in the centre would have seen the lower edge of the sun pass just one half of a degree above the top of the Heel Stone. The findings of Professor Thom, who has made the most careful astro-archaeological surveys to date, show that the main axis of the sarsen circle pointed to the summer sunrise when half its orb was visible over the horizon. Hawkins (apparently ignoring the fact that over almost 4,000 years the surface of the land had been significantly eroded) recalculated the position of this effect. Assuming that the stone was upright, he concluded that at sunrise on the summer solstice the rising Sun would just graze the tip of the Heel Stone as it moved upwards and over.

As Hawkins reveals, the more erratic swing of the Moon is also recorded by the pattern of stones, though in a more complex way since the Moon has a different pattern. Over a period of 18 years and nine months (18.61 years), its rising swings from the north to the south declinations (from 29 degrees to 19 degrees, and then back to 29 degrees), exhibiting two extremes. We find, then, that Diodorus Siculus's account of the spherical temple may have been mistaken in one detail: the periodicity was not specific to the Sun but to the Moon. He might more accurately have recorded that every 19 years the Sun Temple of the Hyperboreans was visited by Luna (not for the Romans an especially important goddess in the spiritual hierarchies).

Whatever his errors, Hawkins had all the amazed sense of wonder of any good pioneer, and he recognised the placement of a 35-ton stone as a truly astounding accomplishment. The sinking of such a giant into the ground, 'just so far and not further, so that its tip was also aligned vertically to an accuracy of inches, was an achievement requiring another whole dimension of skill'.

BURIAL CHAMBERS OR ASTRONOMICAL MACHINES?

Recent research into what have been dubbed 'astro-megalithic structures' has suggested that the ancient past was very different from what is generally believed, in that our forefathers were more interested in studying the stars than in building tombs. The sites and structures classified until now as 'burial grounds' and 'funerary buildings' are being revealed as complex and sophisticated astronomical machines.

Perhaps the most obvious example of the use of megalithic stone-building to reveal solar orientation is that in Newgrange, in Ireland. The use of these ancient Celtic chambers and stones as calendrical instruments is shown in the well argued *The Stars and the Stones* (1983) by Martin Brennan, a man who has worked with special diligence on the Newgrange chamber. In collaboration with Jon Patrick's surveys, he notes that a beam of light passes along this long chamber to strike the backstone in the end recess when the Sun is in a particular position. This position is reached only when the Sun's declination lies between 22 58' and 25 53', and when its azimuth range is 133 42' to 138 24', and when its elevation lies between 0 51' and 1 40'. The elevation of the horizon at Newgrange is 0 51', and this means that it is possible for a beam of light from the sunrise at winter solstice to pass the length of the chamber and so strike the backstone. The general fact that the Newgrange chamber was constructed to permit the rising midsummer Sun to send its rays into the chamber has actually been recognised for some decades. Writing in the 1930s, the anthroposophist Eugene Kolisko remarked that if 'one sits by the altar in the darkness and looks through the small opening at the end of the passage one gets the impression of looking at a star through a long telescope'. He came to the conclusion that the chamber, 'which so much resembles the so-called grave of Atreus in Mycenae', should be described as a temple. Certainly, not a great deal of research is required for one to establish without doubt that a large number of the 'passage graves' and stone circles are linked with solar and lunar orientations, for which one would presume some religious motivation in the minds of their designers. Even apparently 'accidental' boulders and menhirs appear to be markers when examined with sufficient care. As early as 1912, the hillcrest boulder on South Uist, in the Hebrides, was shown to mark the point of sunrise at the winter solstice when viewed from a barrow called Barp. This orientation from barrow to boulder, or to more carefully sited menhir, is by no means uncommon.

It is easy to pass from these observations to the conclusion that many of the so-called 'burial chambers' of the ancient world had nothing to do with mortuary rites, but everything to do with life-related rituals connected with the stars and other cosmic phenomena. The occultist Rudolf Steiner, while making a visit to the Druid's Circle at Penmaenmawr in Wales, indicated that they were used in former times for the observation of phenomena connected with such things as solar radiations, optical sciences and meteorology. Even if the psychic methods used by men like Steiner to determine such things is not considered reliable in modern times, at least one thing is sure – that a whole new field of astro-megalithic research is gradually being opened up. It will demonstrate without a shadow of doubt that the ancient megalithic builders were conversant with astrological and astronomical laws and possessed a wisdom of the highest order. In some ways it is irrelevant what the occultists and mythologizers claim for the origin of these stones – whether they were constructed by giants, or by men with some gigantic and secret power, or whether, as Blavatsky puts it, 'most of these stones are the relics of the last Atlanteans'. We already have enough evidence to show that at the very least, we must reassess all we know of the prehistoric world of man.

Are Stonehenge and related circles, tumuli and burial mounds places where rituals connected with the solar-lunar events were enacted? Did a god or goddess descend into the circle, either in some spiritual form (overshadowing the stone-made structure which itself echoed the shape of the celestial body) or into temporary incarnation, as the ancient myths declare the gods would do from time to time? Or is there an ever-present influx of especially potent stellar forces which invite equivalent earth-forces to strive upwards in a perpetual swell of natural and mysteriously-healing power? Clairvoyants and sensitives are often compelled to admit the spiritual power of most stone circles: I have known people receive a frisson, much like a light electric shock, when touching certain stones of the larger circles, such as Avebury and Stonehenge. What is this power? Does it relate to something which is now lost to Man, and which is remembered only in the garbled tales of the Atlanteans and their extraordinary power of Vril (see page 146)? Or does it relate to a power which Mankind will begin to appreciate and use constructively only in years to come?

The circle of uprights at Penmaenmawr, in Wales, was built (according to local tradition) by the Druids, and is still often referred to as the Druid Circle. However, there is no historical evidence that any stone circles were constructed by Druids, though they may have used them for their own purposes. The majority of British stone circles antedate the Druids by well over two thousand years.

THE STRANGE POWER OF STONES

Before Stonehenge and the other stone circles were subjected to astro-mythological theories (begun in earnest by Theosophists such as Blavatsky, and reaching a flowering with Hawkins), it was widely believed that the circles had been constructed by giants or by magicians. Surely only giants could have carried the stones to build Stonehenge from Wales or Ireland. (Some Theosophists even insisted that these giants were the early Atlanteans.) Alternatively, it has been suggested that Wizards such as Merlin, or Myddyn, had the stones specially flown to the sites from distant mountains.

If the writings of the ancients are to be taken even only partly seriously, we must accept that our ancestors had a different view of stones to that generally held today: for example, they believed that some stones were alive, or at least had been charged with a special virtue by means of magical rituals. The historian and mythologiser Giraldus Cambrensis writes of the magical stone on the Island of Mona which was said to return, of its own accord, to its own place whenever moved from it. The story goes that at the time of the first conquest of Ireland by the English, one Count Hugo Cestrensis, seeking to determine the truth behind this legend, tied the Mona Stone to a far bigger one and had the pair thrown into the sea. On the following morning it was found in its accustomed place. The notion of moving, speaking and self-perambulating stones is very ancient. The rocking stones which are still found in various parts of the country (and which, generally, are now no longer capable of motion), are said by the occultists to have been used in earlier times for divination; hence, their designation as 'the stones of truth'. The most famous of the British rocking stones is the Logan Stone of Cornwall, and history shows that this did not cease its motion until the eighteenth century when it was prised from its delicate position and sent careering into the sea.

As Blavatsky points out, these rocking, or Logan, stones have many names. The Celts had their *clachabrath*, the Destiny or Judgement-stone, the 'stone of the ordeal' or divining stones, and the oracle stone; the Phoenicians their moving or animated stone (remembered even by the Roman historian Pliny). Brittany has its *pierres branlantes* at Huelgoat. Pliny also speaks of several in Asia, whilst the Greek poet Apolonius Rhodius explains that they are 'stones placed on the apex of a tumulus, and so sensitive as to be moveable by the mind'. He might have added 'of those who know the secrets of such stones', by will-power and from a distance.

The most startling of the claims made by occultists is that not only the 'sacred circles', such as those at Callanish and Stonehenge, were built by the ancients, but that so too were many of the outlandish stone formations which are now regarded as natural. Such examples are found on Bodmin Moor, above the stone circles now called the Hurlers, near Minions. The most famous single formation among this particular complex is the Cheesewring, which plays an important part in local mythology. Blavatsky called such sites 'Dracontia, sacred to the moon and the serpent', and she notes that the rocking stones in particular were sacred to the ancients for their motion 'was a code perfectly clear to the initiated priests, who alone had the key to this ancient reading'. The examples of rocking stones at 'Brinham Rocks' (as Blavatsky calls the extensive outcrops of Brimham Rocks, in Yorkshire) are 'evidently the relics of Atlanteans'. She reminds us that some medieval occultists recognised the fact that many such rocks were supposed to have the power of volitional movement, even of speech. Olaus Magnus, the sixteenth-century Swedish historian, wrote of them as oracles, and claimed that the kings of Scandinavaia were elected according to the stone oracles, 'whose voice spoke through the immense rocks raised by the colossal powers of the ancient giants'. Not only vast magical stones were reputed to have the power of speech, but also certain smaller ones, which were worn in the form of amulets. Eusebius of Emesa, who called them his 'snake stones' or ophites, carried some next to his bosom 'and received oracles from them, delivered in a small voice resembling a low whistling'.

The famous Stone of Scone at Westminster, once kept beneath the chair of the Speaker, was once called 'liafail', which meant 'the speaking stone', pointing to the survival of at least one esoteric or magical notion even into modern politics. This indicates that originally, when magical practices were still recognised by the esoteric groups who controlled the destiny of nations, the Speaker was probably the one who understood and translated the sacred voice of the stone. It is not too imaginative to view

Brimham Rocks, in Yorkshire, is a motley collection of eroded rock formations and outcroppings. Archaeological finds indicate that in the past the area was thought to be sacred and it is possible that some of the more outlandish rock forms were worshipped.

Westminster as a huge secular temple, built to house a magical stone, similar to the ones which Olaus Magnus mentions as determining divine rulership.

According to some occultists, the ancient giants who figure in mythology and in the occultist version of history, were a race of early Atlanteans. To them it seems reasonable to assume that such vast megalithic undertakings as the building of Stonehenge were done by superhumans or by wizardry. Blavatsky quotes the strange De Mirville, who 'inquires very pertinently' why the monstrous stones of Stonehenge were in days of old called 'choirgaur' (from *cor* meaning dance, whence chorea, and *gaur*, a giant), or 'the dance of giants'. In 1663 the ancient terminology was revived in the title 'Chorea Gigantum' as one of the names given to *Stone-heng, Standing on Salisbury Plain, Restored to the Danes* by Walter Charleton.

THE LITERARY INFLUENCE OF STONEHENGE

Before that time, Stonehenge had already had a chequered history at the hands of imaginative writers. Even before its structure was wrongly linked with the Druids, it had been posited as a memorial to the Britons killed by Hengist, and, a little later, as a vast tomb to the heroine Boudicca. By the seventeenth century the stones were believed to have been sited by either the Danish (as a Royal court for the election of their kings), or by the Romans, or the Phoenicians. It was William Stukeley who placed the edifice even further back in time and linked the Druids with Stonehenge, even though he was entirely ignorant of the true history of this group and their rites.

Inigo Jones's plan of Stonehenge, which he drew up in 1655, is said to have influenced the architectural design which John Wood executed at the Circus, in Bath.

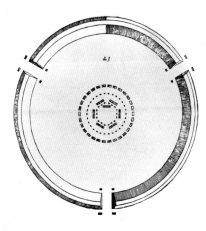

Since then, the circle has had a curious influence on architecture and literature, for, as Stuart Piggott has shown, the architect John Wood (designer of the circus at Bath) based his plans on reconstructions provided by Inigo Jones in 1655. The access from Brock Street, Gay Street, and the short road to the Assembly Rooms reflect the three main entrances to the circle of earthworks visualised by Jones. The most important literary influence which Stukeley had was on William Blake, who adopted the circle in several of his prints and drawings as a symbol of 'National Religion', in which the daughters of Albion tortured their victims. (Blake had accepted the popular notion that Druids used to practise human sacrifice.) Perhaps the most famous image is that in Blake's esoteric work *Jerusalem*, which shows the full Moon central to a massive trilithon, under which stand the robed figures of Bacon, Newton and Locke. The last line of the poem relating to this picture reads:

The Starry Heavens all were fled from the mighty limbs of Albion.

An illustration by William Blake to his esoteric poem *Jerusalem*. Bacon, Newton and Locke, who in Blake's view opposed the imagination natural to man, can be seen under a massive trilithion at Stonehenge.

Another of Blake's engravings of Stonehenge. This view is entirely imaginary, for Blake's Stonehenge is placed on a hill with two avenues of stones running off into a valley.

By this he means that the true imagination of the soul was gone from England. In the last illustration to the poem, this Druidic symbolism is presented again, but with a more hopeful conclusion. It is linked with one of Blake's most enduring symbols, the 'Stone of Night', an emblem of the Druidic doctrine of revenge which is enclosed within the coil of the Serpent Temple (Stonehenge), itself overhung with purple flowers and deadly nightshade. Also depicted are his creatures Los, carrying hammer and tongs, Vala ('Her name is Vala in Eternity: in Time her name is Rahab') with the crescent Moon, and the Sun-bearing Luvah.

This Blakean Stonehenge is uncompromisingly serpentine, for from the main circle emerges a tail of stones which spirals off in a coil beneath the feet of sun-bearing Luvah. A second spiral curves off into the earth beneath the crescent Moon, suggesting that the Druidic circle is now linked with the spiritual realm, with Sun and Moon. As in all matters of symbolism, Blake is entirely personal in his esoteric references, yet the image of the Sun to the left of the image, and crescent Moon to the right (derived from religious and occult symbols), and that of the stars in the void above the circle of stone, may be taken as prophetic. His notions about the purpose of Stonehenge predate those of today – that it is a repository of cosmic and calendrical wisdom.

STONES AND WATER

In this 'Celtic image', Gordon Wain has combined a striking image of the chalk hill-figure of a horse at Uffington (which many occultists claim was originally a dragon) with a view of the burial mound known as Wayland's Smithy.

The tendency in modern times has been for investigators to look towards the heavens in search of the key to the ancient mysteries of the stone circles, mounds and burial tombs which are found throughout the British Isles. Yet builders who could take into account the periodicities of the Sun and Moon, and perhaps even those planets known at the time might also be able to take into account patterns engendered by the secret powers of the earth itself. This, at least, was one of the guiding theories of Guy Underwood when he undertook to investigate many of the ancient sites, sacred places and hill figures. He used a series of sophisticated dowsing techniques, designed to reveal the geoforces which were presumably recognised by the ancients. In the published results of this research (the fascinating book, *Patterns of the Past*), Underwood looked *beneath* the earth for the secrets of Stonehenge, rather than into the stars. He pointed out that many of the strange formations of the stones may be explained in terms of the earth-currents or geolines in the area of Stonehenge. Underwood has also published many dowsing maps of the geolines which may be determined by underground springs and other earth currents. Very often these explain in a most interesting way the genesis of stone circles, the positions of dolmens and even the shapes of such gigantic hill figures as the White Horse (in fact, a Dragon) at Uffington, in Berkshire.

With specific regard to Stonehenge, Underwood has observed that stone 51 of the horseshoe complex was sunk over a blind spring. (A blind spring is the underground confluence of two streams, which may be mapped out by dowsing techniques.) Such springs are very often signalled by ancient mark-points, such as dolmens, monoliths and so on. Stone 51 had a hole of approximately 4 inches in diameter and 2 feet in depth bored into the top, and this was always filled with water, never drying away completely even during periods of drought. For cleaning purposes, the hole was syphoned off from time to time, yet it would quickly fill up with clear water. Sadly, the hole has been filled with cement in modern times, and the ancient magic no longer works.

Reflecting on this strange phenomenon, in an interesting article on the magical nature of ancient dew ponds, Paul Baines suggested that the stone and its lintel were intended as a condenser to provide a small but permanent supply of water, perhaps for ritual purposes. The use of sacred springs for ritual purposes is well attested in ancient literature, but one of the most remarkable survivals from the past is the lovely chapel of St Clether in Cornwall, which has a stream running directly beneath the altar. Many of the ancient healing wells required total immersion (as in the old baptismal methods) for complete success to be possible, suggesting that the healing power resided in the water as much as in the ritual. In other words, it is possible that the ancients believed that some kinds of water had secret properties which were different from other kinds of water; that there was such a thing as 'therapeutic, or healing water'.

The ancients regarded dew and even rainwater as possessing quite extraordinary qualities, and went to great lengths to collect it in pure form. In particular, the alchemists believed that dew contained within it natural vital forces which were of great importance to their work, and one finds in their texts many detailed accounts of how best to collect it. A most interesting illustration of one such technique is found in the *Mutus Liber*, widely circulated as an enigmatic, alchemical manuscript prior to the seventeenth century but not printed until 1677. In this book, which is probably the strangest of all esoteric books published in La Rochelle, we find the alchemists collecting dew with the aid of clean sheets stretched over four posts. The saturated cloths are squeezed dry by a simple twisting procedure: it would seem that a man and a woman are important in this ritual, for above them, in the cosmic equivalent of the heavens, we see the Sun on the male side of the operation and the Moon on the female side. The plate suggests that the pair are not merely collecting water, for the stream of forces down into the world below indicates that the dew must contain within it some cosmic power which will be of value to the alchemists; it also indicates that the

A plate from the *Mutus Liber*, showing the ritual collection of heavenly dew.

collecting of this mysterious liquid must take place at the appropriate cosmic moment, for the Ram of Aries is on the left, and the Bull of Taurus on the right. We could interpret the symbolism as suggesting that the collecting must be done when the Sun is between Aries and Taurus, or when the Sun is in Aries (since the Sun is on the left hand side of the plate) and the Moon in Taurus (since the bull is on the lunar side of the plate). In either case, the collecting should be done near to the beginning of spring, for each of these two alternatives place the important time in the month of April, formerly the month of Aries, standing at the beginning of the old calendar. Other plates in the *Mutus Liber* show what stages the alchemist must follow in the treatment of his magical dew in order to attain his spiritual aims.

Surely there is something common both to these occult theories of solar-lunar cycles and to the strange imagery of the *Mutus Liber*; something which reflects a much later occult stream of thinking. On the one hand, a solar being named Apollo descends to earth, presumably at the request of the Stonehenge initiates: the spherical temple which he overshadows, or into which he becomes incarnate, is designed to reflect solar and lunar cycles, and is almost certainly linked with a life-giving cult of the stars. On the other hand, the image of the dew collecting in Plate Four of the *Mutus Liber* shows a spiritual power pouring to earth, the Sun and Moon involved in the operation, and even marks a specific moment in the calendar. Just as the ancient initiates would gather something of spiritual worth from the visit of Apollo, so the alchemist-Rosicrucians gain something of inestimable value from the heavenly dew which they collect. The shared notion is that man receives sustenance from the heavenly realms, and that this sustenance may be obtained only through special ritual or invocation. This is the basic rule of the esoteric tradition.

It is perhaps of only passing interest that some of the ancients believed that the moon goddess Selene and the leader of the Gods, Zeus, were the parents of Herse, the dew, and that in virtually all the ancient occult systems the Moon is linked with water, tides and dew. Is there any connection between these old beliefs and Stonehenge? And was the esotericist William Blake aware of these connections when, on the left of his image of Stonehenge, he gave a radiant solar life to the globe on Luvah's shoulder, and does rain, or perhaps dew, stream from the crescent moon to its right?

MYSTERIOUS ALIGNMENTS

To the north of Carnac in Brittany is the largest stone alignment in Europe – perhaps, indeed, in the entire world. The 4,000 prehistoric menhirs, some over 20 feet high, are grouped into four approximate areas along four kilometres of the D196 road. To the south-west is the le Ménec group, further north-east is the Kermario group, and to the north-east of this are the smaller Kerlescant and Petit-Ménec stones. Among the Kermario uprights is the extraordinary Kermario Dolmen, which is said to be far older than the alignments themselves. The Ménec group still consists of hundreds of stones set in 11 parallel rows, yet there may be no doubt that for all the complexity of such surviving alignments, the stones were once far more numerous.

The long alignment of uprights at Ménec, north of Carnac, which has been dated to about 2,400 BC, is set in eleven parallel rows. The Carnac site is said to be the largest prehistoric structure in Europe.

An early scholar, working on archaeological surveys, estimated that in ancient times well over 10,000 stones were raised in this part of Brittany, and some specialists appear prepared to double that estimate. The extraordinary thing is that there seems to have been no historical mention of the Carnac stones before the eighteenth century, when a member of the Academy of Sciences reported their presence and noted that the local peasants believed that certain of them had the power to heal and protect their cattle.

The German equivalent of Carnac is not in the form of man-aligned stones, but rather in the form of man-carved rocks. This fascinating centre of ancient German esotericism is an outlandish chain of sandstone rocks, on the northern slopes of the Teutoburg forest, called the Externsteine. They are part-natural in formation, part-carved by man. The most important of the 12 main formations are those located on either side of the road which has been driven through them in relatively modern times. The two rocks to the north, immediately at the side of the road, are connected by a steep staircase which terminates in a bridge leading to an upper chapel. In this is an altar, above which is a porthole window so orientated as to permit the rays of the solstice sunrise to fall upon the centre of the alcove at the back of the chapel. As we may see from our study of solar orientation in chapter 4, it is not uncommon for the ancients to have made use of solstitial sunlight effects, but the reasons for this orientation at the Externsteine is unknown. However, it has been suggested that the prophetess Veleda, from the Bructerian tribe of the lower Rhine, lived in the upper cave or sanctuary, and it may have been for her benefit that the porthole was carved. The sun, rising over the high horizon of distant hills, would have projected a level beam of light through this sanctuary, perhaps to fall upon Veleda's face at the summer solstice.

The huge rock to the south of this road is crowned by a large balancing rock, which in relatively recent times was stabilised with the aid of iron grips and a concrete bedding. It seems, however, that this stabilising was quite unnecessary as the rocking stone had been in place for millennia. The eastern face of this rock contains a partly 'natural' and partly man-made image of a man with outstretched hands, which is usually interpreted as the pagan god Odin, hanging, as though crucified, upon the rock surface. This image reminds us that Odin willingly undertook to hang for nine days upon the Yggdrasil tree – the sacred tree of Norse mythology – in order to gain the secret wisdom of the ancients. The body of this figure has been gashed, no doubt to remind the onlooker that while Odin hung on the tree, his body was pierced by a spear.

One of the rock-faces across the road, to the north, has taken the Christian version of this theme and, in the early twelfth century, craftsmen carved upon its surface a huge relief depicting Christ's descent from the cross. Although the relief is mutilated, it is still possible to see Joseph of Arimathea taking down the body of Christ: he is standing on what may at first appear to be a curious chair. In fact, this is not a chair at all but the pagan Irminsul, the ancient mystic tree of Teutonic mystery religions, represented here as bowing down in recognition of the new mystery wisdom of the Christ.

Some writers have insisted that before the eighth century, a huge representation of the Irminsul stood on top of the rock which now bears the image of the crucified Christ. According to quasi-historical legends derived from the Carolingian period, this huge Irminsul was removed in AD 772 on the orders of Charlemagne. This ancient tree, the form of which is found even among the runes, is linked with the Nordic Yggdrasil, and was so intimately associated with German pagan nationalism that during the brief period of Nazi supremacy in Germany, Himmler planned to replace the Irminsul, like a vast sigil for the zodiacal sign Aries, upon the pinnacle of this rock.

The rocks of Externsteine contain many natural and man-made caves. While it is difficult to give a date when these were first used for mystical practices, some archaeologists believe that the 'inset tomb', near the edge of the artificial lake, is at least 5,000 years old. They go on to claim that it is not a tomb at all, but an ancient initiation chamber rather like that inside the Dwarfie Stone on the island of Hoy in the Orkneys. The space for the body is orientated on an east-west line, with the legs directed towards the point of sunrise; while the location of the cave in which the body is placed is directed towards the north — a quite unnatural place for burial, but one ideal for initiation purposes.

A view from the west towards Externsteine, showing the approach to the chapel cut in the rock, into which the first rays of the solstice sunrise pierce, through a specially carved porthole.

The Kermario alignment to the north-east of Carnac. Specialists have calculated that once there must have been well over 10,000 upright menhirs in the Carnac site, but some authorities are prepared to double this number.

The huge natural formation at Externsteine which portrays the god Odin hanging on the Yggdrasil tree, sacred in Norse and Germanic mythology. His bowed head and outstretched arms may be seen halfway down the rock.

THE BLENDING OF DIFFERENT TRADITIONS

The manner in which the Externsteine imagery combined pagan and Christian elements may be astonishing to modern eyes, for we are accustomed nowadays to separating quite clearly in our minds the Christian realm from the world of pagan beliefs. However, in medieval times this separation was not so rigid, and we find that many of the secret centres of Europe use symbolic programmes which merge pagan mythology, Druidic symbolism and so on, with thoroughly Christian images.

Among the French cathedrals where this mingling is most evident are those at Chartres and Amiens; the former being rich in astrological and mythological imagery, the latter combining alchemical and astrological symbolism of a very abstruse kind. It is no wonder that both these cathedrals have become famous among occultists interested in secret symbols.

Chartres appears to have been the centre of initiation symbolism for at least two esoteric groups. The first was linked ultimately with the Druids, and the second group was derived from a Christian school of the twelfth century which sought to combine the wisdom of the early church with the astrological lore of the Arabs (something which at that time was fascinating scholars in the West). The very name of Chartres is said to be derived from the Druidic language, for the early Celtic tribes that settled in Central Gaul were called the Carnutes, and the hill town adopted as their Mystery Centre was called Carnutum. It is from this name that the modern word is derived, and it was almost certainly this town which Julius Caesar had in mind when he wrote, in his *Gallic Wars*, of 'a consecrated spot' at the centre of the whole land of the Gauls, where those who were in dispute came to accept the judgements of the Druids. The Carnutes were not the original founders of Chartres, however, for, long before their own rise to power, that part of Europe which we now call France had been settled by a group of people traditionally called the Gomerites. These, according to tradition, were led by the first king and lawgiver of the post-Atlantean flood, Samotes, and it was they who founded the hill village which became modern Chartres.

Modern occultists claim that the ancient sanctuary cave beneath Chartres cathedral, which has now been incorporated into the crypt, was originally Druidic; but there is some evidence to suggest that it predates even the Druids as a centre of Mystery Wisdom, and was linked with the Gomerites. That a sacred cave was there before the Christians erected their first church (long before the cathedral was built) is widely recognised, as is the fact that in this cave was one of the most important of the Black Virgin statues associated with the Druidic sacred lore.

Legend tells how, immediately after the death of Christ, two of his followers who set out to preach the Gospel journeyed to Gaul. When they arrived at Carnutum, thinking themselves the first Christians to set foot in that part of the world, they discovered it was already Christian. The ancient sanctuary had already been rededicated to the Virgin of the new Mystery Wisdom. The explanation given for this change of dedication was that the Druid priests, long familiar with the destiny of the Earth, had seen in visions the ministry and death of Christ, and had recognised the purpose of His coming. It was even told in ancient records that the Druids, aware of the impending birth of Jesus, had sent three ambassadors to seek out the Virgin Mary and ask her to take the name of 'Lady of Carnutum'. The Druidic, and therefore 'pagan' black madonna (which, in modern times, has been called the 'black Isis') thus became Christian because the Druids recognised that their own brand of esotericism was fulfilled in the new mystery wisdom of Christianity.

The story of the Black Virgin has been investigated many times in recent years, and Ean Begg has produced a useful gazetteer of European sites where such images may be seen in *The Cult of the Black Virgin* (1985). However, not all the virgins claimed for this tradition were originally black. For example, the beautiful twelfth-century image called Our Lady of Miracles (in Notre-Dame-des-Miracles at Mauriac) still bears on its surface the tell-tale traces of gold, indicating its original colour. In spite of this, and in spite of the fact that there are numerous similar images in French churches, we may not doubt that in some cases the tradition of the Black Virgin is rooted in an hermetic reality. It requires no strong imagination to see the influence of this Black Virgin of pre-Christian lore in the dark-faced Madonna of thirteenth-century stained-glass window.

Towards the end of the French Revolution, which did so much to destroy and desecrate the mystery wisdom still intact in the old cathedrals of France, the mysterious 'Lady of the Crypt', which was of the Black Virgin type, was removed and burned publicly in the square to the south of the cathedral. Just as the Druids had been stamped out by the material power of Rome, so the link with the mystery past was stamped out by the materialistic power of the New Enlightenment thinking. The Black Madonna now on display in the crypt is a replacement, carved in 1857. However, this does not mean that all the mystery-lore of ancient Chartres has been lost: even today examples of esoteric and occult symbolism may be found on the sculptural programme on the west front of the cathedral.

This symbolic programme was worked out by architects and designers at a most important moment in the history of Europe, when the learning of the ancient world – preserved by Arabic scholars in such centres as Baghdad, Damascus, Cairo and parts of Islamic Spain – was being transmitted, translated and appreciated by influential Western thinkers. One of the main reasons for this injection of new knowledge was the contact between Christianity and Islam established during Crusades, but the presence of a powerful Islamic presence in Spain also helped facilitate this process. Among the new sciences eagerly studied by Western scholars was astrology, which had been developed by Arabic scholars to a level of perfection rarely seen afterwards. The Arabs had taken the astrological learning of the classical world, and refined it with their own special approach to star-lore, mathematics and symbolism. During the twelfth and thirteenth centuries the star lore of the West was so poor that scholars were keen to grasp what the Arabs had to offer, and, since this time corresponded to the vast expansion of church and cathedral building, symbols derived from the new astrology were incorporated into the façades and interiors of many new buildings.

Examples abound in the area formerly dominated by the Druids, but the most notable are found in the astrological programme of Notre-Dame, Paris, and on the façade of Notre-Dame in Chartres. In fact, the best known of the esoteric elements at Chartres is not the extensive programme of astrological imagery in stone and stained glass, but the maze – something which has given rise to the most absurd theories in hermetic literature.

There was a time when many mazes were to be found in the floors of many churches and cathedrals in Europe, but time, which defaces most things, has taken its toll and few of these remain. The most beautiful are undoubtedly those at Chartres and Ely. The Chartres example is not, strictly speaking, a maze at all since the passageway

The beautifully preserved maze in Ely cathedral is a reminder that in medieval times many churches and cathedrals had internal mazes. It has been proposed by some occultists that these mazes were actually dancing grounds, where a penitent or pilgrim would dance, or perhaps crawl on his knees, from the outer edge to the centre, to the holy place where the peace of god was found.

This Greek bowl of the fifth century, BC, shows the killing of the Cretan Minotaur by the hero Theseus.

which circles its undulating course does not permit anyone to get lost. This fact has led some historians to regard it as a dancing ground in which the celebrant sets out on the journey along the pathway, perhaps in a state of meditation, centring himself as he approaches the middle. The pathway thus becomes a symbolic progression towards the 'centre' which is God.

The only argument against this theory is that originally the centre of the maze bore a metal plaque on which was inscribed not an image of God, but of Theseus and the Minotaur – a thoroughly pagan image. The classical story of the Athenian who sought out and killed the bull-headed Minotaur in the maze at Knossos is preserved in another very interesting medieval maze, now set in the wall of the cathedral in Lucca, in Italy. The Latin inscription alongside this crudely-cut maze (the form of which reminds us of the Chartres circle) does not mention the Minotaur, but it does refer to the maze in Crete, built by Daedalus, and reminds us that Theseus found his way out of the labyrinth thanks to Ariadne. Perhaps it is in this female name that we may trace a meaningful relationship between the maze and Christian thought, for the dance towards the centre may be interpreted as a dance towards the place where the archetypal woman (the Virgin Mary) rescues the one lost (the dancer) from the clutches of the Devil (the horned bull so reminiscent of the horned Devil).

While the mazes of European churches and cathedrals have largely disappeared now, many French, Italian and German churches and cathedrals sport large numbers of occult symbols, the most arcane ones being connected with alchemy. This, perhaps, is not all that surprising, as in the medieval period alchemy received almost as much attention as astrology. Medieval alchemy, rather like medieval astrology, was deeply concerned with the use of symbols as 'philosophical machines', as what we might nowadays call revelations of the archetypes. In the guise of alchemy's 'chemical processes' the medieval adepts saw a perfect system for presenting the various stages of a human being's spiritual development through inner disciplines and meditations. Alchemical and Christian symbolism are intimately connected, therefore, and one has to be alert to subtle variations even to sense the difference between the two.

Some individuals dedicated themselves to searching for a way to make the substance of gold, but there were also esoteric or hermetic groups wholly dedicated to using alchemical systems as a means of approaching spiritual perfection. We find in many medieval cities records in stone of such highly-spiritualised aims. In Florence, for example, in the splendid Signoria (which vies with the cathedral to dominate the city's

A medieval maze on an external wall of Lucca cathedral, in Italy, carved in the thirteenth century. Once again, it is not a true maze, but a circuitous passage which leads gradually but inexorably to the centre. This design is similar to the large marble maze on the floor of the nave at Chartres cathedral.

skyline), we find a small room with exotic frescoes wholly given over to complex alchemical symbols. Similarly, in the beautiful moated château of Plessis-Bourré in the Loire valley, built by Jean Bourré, a minister of Louis XI who was interested in occultism and alchemy, the guardroom has a coffered wooden ceiling that features many hermetic symbols relating to the spagyric art. In the church at Dampierre-sur-Boutonne, the first word of which evokes the philsopher's stone (*Dame Pierre*, the Stone of the Virgin), ceiling sculptures of the sixteenth century are also derived from alchemical symbolism.

We have already noted some of the zodiacal symbols on the façade of the cathedral at Amiens, and so it will be instructive to examine one or two of the alchemical and occult images from the same structure. The most obvious of all these is that of the secret liquid, sometimes called the Philosophers' Dew. It is found in a curious quartrefoil in the Porch of the Virgin Mother, which some have called the 'alchemical porch'. Before the astonished gaze of an alchemist, this celestial dew pours down from the clouds which, in medieval iconography, represented the heavens, and lands all around him. The modern alchemist Fulcanelli interprets this as an image of nostoc. This name was coined by another alchemist, Paracelsus, who derived it from the Greek word for night. It is also used to describe unicellular algae which arranges itself in intertwining rows to form a gelatinous mass. Properly speaking nostoc is a vegetable with no stamens or pistils: it swells in the morning dew, but vanishes with the sun's rays. In medieval times it was believed that this mysterious plant was an emanation from the stars, and Fulcanelli gives many alternative names for it, including Heavenly Flower and Moon-Spit, and points out that the symbolism of nostoc was of great importance to the alchemical tradition. We have seen this heavenly dew in another context, in the alchemical imagery of the Rosicrucians.

The beautiful moated château of Plessis-Bourré, in the Loire valley, where the guardroom has a coffered ceiling filled with images of the alchemical and occult arts.

Detail from the façade of the cathedral at Amiens, showing the fall of the Philosopher's Dew, which the modern alchemist, Fulcanelli, called nostoc.

The southern porch of the west front at Amiens cathedral, which is known as the Alchemical Porch because of its enormous collection of arcane, alchemical symbols.

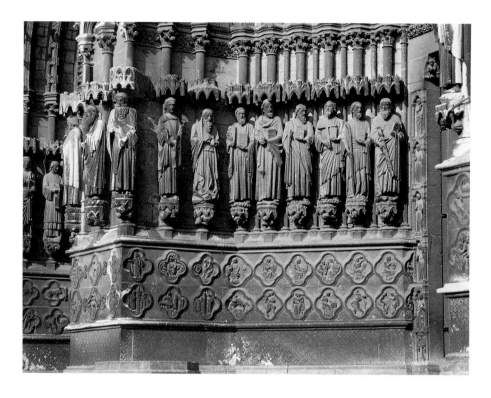

A detail of one of the quatrefoils from the Alchemical Porch at Amiens, showing the curious revolving wheel, which is an impossible union of two intertwined wheel rims. The image is probably derived from the alchemical notion that the manufacture of the philosopher's stone requires a double motion, a fast one and a slow one, each in opposite directions.

The fall of the dew creates the ephemeral night vegetable and represents the rebirth which takes place in every man during the period of sleep. If this dew represents the period return of a life-force, what does the nostoc itself symbolize? It must, indeed, represent the human being himself, the ephemeral creature of the stars, the Heavenly Flower which comes to earth at night by way of the stars, when the influence of the Moon is at its height, but which disappears when burned by the sun. The symbolism which links birth with the Moon and decomposition with the Sun is perhaps even older than alchemy, for it is rooted in the occult tradition.

It is perhaps no accident that some occultists have interpreted the Amiens nostoc as a representation of the Golden Fleece which hung on an oak tree in Colchis, guarded by a dragon. The Golden Fleece was another of the alchemists' symbols, who saw in it a suitable emblem for the sacred thing which they sought, and which they knew to be guarded by a dragon. Here, again, we see the way in which the medieval symbolists chose to hide their Christian meanings behind the outer garb of classical mythology. Just as Ariadne was a prototype for the Virgin Mary, and the Minotaur a prototype of the Devil, so the dragon of Colchis is the Devil and the Golden Fleece the treasure of Christian life.

There are many other alchemical symbols at Amiens, but the nostoc, created by the heavenly dew, is probably the one which is most expressive of the strange relevance of alchemical thought to everyday life. However, the image of the intertwined wheel rims, in a quite impossible union, is so complex as to be almost beyond explanation. The double wheel represents a medieval alchemical belief that one process in the manufacture of the secret stone demands a double motion (one slow, the other fast) in opposite directions. How else might one symbolise this strange imagery in stone save by means of two inter-related wheels with nine spokes each? The two sets of spokes together total 18, which is the number associated with the sequence of eclipses, as well as that of an important astrological period known as the lunar number. This lunar number, so obviously linked with the solar image of the spoked wheel itself, is yet another alchemical reference to the notion of union between Man's two polarities – the female (lunar) element and the masculine (solar). Without such a union, the further alchemical development of the soul and spirit would be impossible.

The mingling of pagan and Christian imagery which seems to be one of the most important elements in the secret symbolism of the cathedrals is also found in much more humble settings throughout Europe.

The houses in Alberobello, southern Italy, are well known for their conical roofs, as well as for the large number of occult, alchemical, astrological and hermetic sigils which are painted on them.

The town of Alberobello, in southern Italy, is a curious place in which a mixture of alchemical, astrological and occult symbolism can be seen in an unusual form. Many of the houses in Alberobello, and in the surrounding countryside, are built with conical roofs, and are called *trulli* (the singular is *trullo*), in a style which is foreign to Europe, though similar examples are occasionally found in southern France. What is of great interest to occultists is the fact that the roofs of some of these houses are painted with magical symbols from the alchemical, astrological and general occult tradition. Some are painted with symbols intended to reflect the names of those who dwell within the building, while others are painted with standard Christian symbols such as the cross, or the dove of peace. In recent years there have been several academic studies of these symbols, and careful copies have been made of the surviving images. Since the symbols are painted in whitewash (sometimes, nowadays, with an acrylic base) they require frequent reworking, and the result is that many of the forms have become obscured,

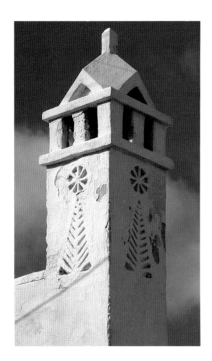

Many of the chimneys on the houses of Mykonos are decorated with esoteric symbols, some of which hark back to pagan themes, while others are clearly Christian.

This Mykonos chimney has a finial in the form of a fish – a Christian symbol for the Christ.

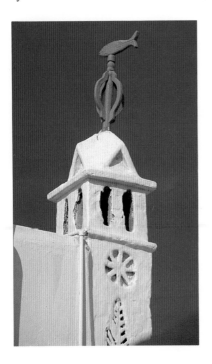

and certain of the original designs lost. Even so, the notes of researchers (such as the Italian historian Verardi) and the survival of many old photographs have made it possible to construct a fairly comprehensive list of the symbols, along with indications, derived mainly from surveys among those who paint them, of their meaning. Almost all those who continue to paint or repaint the *trullo* symbols do so with the belief that they protect the houses themselves in some way, and render them more beneficient as dwellings.

The houses on the island of Mykonos (close to that most sacred of ancient Greek islands, Delos) also has an established system of protective secret symbols. Instead of being painted on the roofs, however, these symbols are built into the chimneys. Their forms vary, but the most common are trees, solar discs and fish, the meanings of which almost certainly go back to ancient mythology, interpreted in the light of modern Christianity.

As we have noted in connection with the Irminsul, the tree has been a sacred symbol in many cults and religions, and at Mykonos we may be tempted to trace it back to the sacred palm under which Apollo, the Sun god, was born. A lone, sacred palm tree is still to be seen among the ruins at Delos, and this is often pointed out as the place where the goddess Leto gave birth to her solar child. The Sun symbols on the chimneys of Mykonos are also related to the Apollo myth, for the word 'Apollo' was used widely in medieval astrological texts as an alternative name for the Sun, and as a deified personification of solar power. Of course, in early times, Christ was also regarded as being a representative of the Sun, and the first Christians clearly saw Him in symbolic form as a continuation of the Apollo symbolism. The halos on the heads of Christ and His saints point to this connection with the solar rays, and in some medieval imagery we find the picture of Christ as a radiant sun surrounded by the 12 disciples, also representative of the 12 signs of the zodiac. The Mykonos symbolism of Sun and Tree can therefore be interpreted as referring to Christ and the Tree (the source of the wooden cross) and so as a symbol of the Redemptive act. Confirmation of this Christian redemptive motif may be seen in the fact that certain of the chimney symbols are topped by carved wooden fishes. The fish is by far the most frequently used of all symbols for Christ, and was first used in the catacombs under Rome in the two or three centuries following His death. The Mykonos symbols are of great interest because it is possible to read, or interpret, their forms in both pagan and Christian terms; it is up to the individual to decide which system of belief to adopt.

Anyone who goes to Mykonos to study the pagan/Christian symbolism of its chimneys would be well devised to take a short boat ride to Delos. Delos was the sacred island of the ancient world, and it is not surprising that a large number of interesting sacred or occult symbols should have survived on its barren-seeming surface. The graffiti is scratched on stones, walls and columns, with images ranging from curious alchemical sigils (for example, on the much-scratched remains of the statue of Apollo) to early Christian inscriptions containing images of fishes, to penis-images favoured in some sacred centres by the Romans. The marble figure of Apollo, which was once the largest in the ancient world, lies in dismembered fragments on the edge of what used to be his temple, where the god was supposed to become incarnate at certain times of the year. These fragments, covered with graffiti symbols in a hundred languages, remind us of the other edge of Europe, of the standing stones near Salisbury where the god was also supposed to become incarnate every 19 years.

Some of the images at Delos remind us of the Romans' preoccupation with phallus worship which they inherited from the Etruscans and, to a lesser extent, the Greeks. The male sexual organ was frequently adopted as an image of spiritual strength from which organic life could be generated in some mysterious and magical way. There is, for example, a most interesting line of such phallic stones, which obviously played a part in the programme of symbolism at some temple. While the phallic images at Delos are quite large, many smaller ones of Roman origin – usually combining the male phallus with bull (Taurean) imagery – have survived as amulets. (It was also a very common practice to incise images of the phallus on the bottom of drinking vessels, in order to convey the magical power of life to the liquid to be drunk.) Many museums have such amulets and drinking-vessel symbols in their collections, but the public display in the museum of

Roman antiquities at Augst in Switzerland is especially interesting.

There may not be much apparent difference between graffito marks and the prehistoric scratches left in the rocks of some European sacred sites, but the difference is actually profound. It is unlikely that prehistoric artists practised their art merely for its own sake, and one has the impression that all the paintings, carvings and graffiti which they left were bound up with magic. The secret magic of the hunt is evident in the superb paintings of Lascaux and in the less artistic cave pictures at Antequera in southern Spain.

One of the most famous of all surface rock carvings is that found among the many hunt-scenes at Capo di Ponte, in northern Italy. This scratched image portrays a man in a curious headdress, which the writer Erich von Daniken in his *In Search of Ancient Gods* had no hesitation in interpretating as a representation of a spaceman wearing a helmet. This theory, which appears to support Daniken's notion that Mankind in earlier times had commerce with space-travellers, is based on a misunderstanding.

Such images emphasising headgear find parallels in the Egyptian sculptures and frescoes depicting gods and goddesses with curious heads, and are very common in ancient forms of art. Examples may be found in South American pre-Columbian art, Chinese, Japanese, Indian, Tibetan, and so on: they are an expression of an important

The mystical island of Delos, a few miles from Mykonos, once the most holy place in the ancient world. This phallic symbol is one of a series which adorn a sacred walk in a temple precinct.

The prehistoric rock carving, made by pitting the smooth surface of a rock with a hard stone or chisel, at Capo di Ponte, in northern Italy.

belief concerning the relationship which Man has with the spiritual world. It was widely held, until comparatively recently, that Mankind lived immersed in a sea of spiritual forces: these spiritual forces were invisible to ordinary men, yet they were varied and ranged from the demonic to the angelic. A further belief was that Man was in tune with this spiritual world through his thinking. It is for this reason that in the mystery wisdom of the Egyptians the different grades of initiation (designed to permit clairvoyant insight into the normally invisible spiritual world) were indicated by certain symbols in the area of the head. Hence the Egyptian gods are animal-headed, or distinguished by such strangely-wrought symbols involving snakes, wings, plants and so on: the headgear, or headform, was an indication of initiation rank. In view of this, and in view of the fact that there is a traceable line of descent from the rock-carvings at such sacred sites as Capo di Ponte, and the images of ancient Egypt, we may take it that the strange headgear of the so-called astronaut has nothing to do with space travel, and is merely an example of magical symbolism.

RUNES AND THE LEGACY OF ATLANTIS

Of all the ancient languages which have been left as stone inscriptions in Europe, the one which has caught the attention of esotericists most, and which has thrilled those interested in various aspects of divination, is the Nordic system of runes. In mythology, at least, it is linked with the oldest of all occult histories – that of Atlantis.

It was the nineteenth-century scholar Ignatius Donnelly who first proposed that Asgard, 'the Scandinavian Olympus' of northern mythology, was Atlantis. Prior to this theory, it was generally believed that Atlantis had been a vast continent occupying the space now covered by the Atlantic, peopled first by giants and then by men of superior wisdom and intellect. Although most of the land disappeared over 14,000 years ago, ancient maps are very clear about its shape and size, and even about the locations of the main cities among its plains and volcanos.

Atlantis was a 'culture' as much as a continent. According to the occult tradition, Atlantis was the sophisticated culture which preceded our own Western one, and to which Plato refers in *Timaeus*. Popular imagination, fed by romantic literature and images from the silver screen, now peoples Atlantis with a race of people not unlike ourselves, with a developed science including airships, terrible weapons and the power of black magic. The serious occultists write of the Atlanteans in different terms however, claiming that they were the ones who conquered the ancient giants of the pre-Atlantean civilisations, and built the first pyramids of which those in Central America and Egypt are merely later copies. They had a secret power over nature which was more formidable than our own, and their civilization was destroyed because they used this power unwisely.

The occult tradition insists that it was the black magic of the evil Atlantean priests, who used natural powers illegally, which brought destruction by water to this continent. However, it is related that thousands of years later their opponents, the white magicians, built the stone circles and raised the mysterious menhirs which still grace the northern parts of Europe.

The maps shown here indicate the extent of the old Atlantis, as the modern occultists describe it. Parts of the Americas were still linked with the vast continent, as were some of the lands to the east, such as the Highlands of Scotland, the Hebrides and some of the mountainous regions of Scandinavia. These are the places where it is claimed the ancient arts of stone circle building (the lifting of enormous menhirs by magical means) and magical writing began long before the birth of Christ. Many of the old myths in these areas have wizards as the builders of the ancient stone circles. These figures had the power to have heavy stones float on air, merely at the sound of a word or at the forming of a magical letter, and are linked with the occultists' tales of the power of the Atlantean wise men.

The chief god of the ancient Nordic mythologies was Odin (called Wotan by the Germanic races), and in his book on Atlantis, Donnelly points out that the Chiapanese of Central America, whose mythology was known only after the sixteenth century and who themselves claim to have been the first race to come to the New World, believed that the grandson of the man who saved humanity from the Flood was called Votan. It

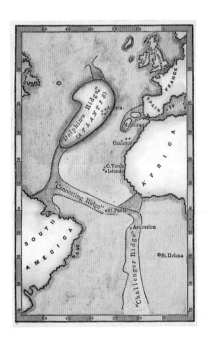

A nineteenth-century map showing the shape of the lost continent of Atlantis, and its position relative to Europe and the Americas.

A seventeenth-century map of Atlantis, together with the two islands later named Ruta and Daiyta. This map was made by the Jesuit polymath Athanasius Kircher, who seemingly based his drawing on classical literary references to the lost continent and islands. From the 1678 edition of *Mundus subterraneus*.

was this Votan who undertook to build a tower which would stretch from earth to heaven, presumably to reunite Mankind with 'the land of the gods that had been lost due to the Flood which overwhelmed Atlantis. According to the legend told in the *Popol vuh*, Votan was ordered to bring seven families to what we now call America, and he built a great city called Nachan, which was the 'City of the Serpents'. There he wrote a history of his deeds – the first history in America.

ATLANTIS: THE LINK WITH EUROPE

The link between the Scandinavian peoples and the fabled founding of the Americas is supported by the famous Piri Reis map, now in the museum at the Topkapi Palace, Istanbul. It is dated 1513, and shows the coastline and islands of the Atlantic which were not known or charted until our own times. Piri Reis was a Turkish admiral and cartographer whose curious map, drawn on gazelle hide, was discovered in fragmentary form in 1929. He claimed to have constructed it from over 20 other available maps – including that used by Christopher Columbus who had returned from his voyage of discovery two years previously. It clearly shows land bridges and islands which (we now know) had been hidden by the sea for thousands of years, and it also contains material which related accurately to the outline of the Antarctic that was not known to us until the Norwegian/British/Swedish Expedition of 1949–52. We are driven to the fascinating speculation that the old maps used in the Piri Reis compilation point to a knowledge of the Americas which was lost before their rediscovery in the late fifteenth century. May we take this as an unexpected confirmation of mythologies tracing the chief Scandinavian god to one of the founding leaders of the Americas?

For the remarkable occultist H. P. Blavatsky, the ancient myths were rooted in historical reality, and the Piri Reis map would probably have caused her no surprise. She claims, indeed, that parts of the Scandinavian peninsula were once linked with Atlantis: '...in the days when tropical nature was found, where now lie eternal unthawing snows, one could cross almost by dry land from Norway via Iceland and Greenland, to the lands that at present surround Hudson's Bay. Just as in the palmy days of the Atlantean giants, the sons of the "giants of the East", a pilgrim could perform a journey from what in our days is termed the Sahara desert, to the lands which now rest in dreamless sleep at the bottom of the waters of the Gulf of Mexico and the Caribbean Sea.'

'This', she adds in a footnote, 'may account for the similarity of the artificial mounds in the United States of America, and the tumuli in Norway. It is this identity that led some American archaeologists to suggest that Norwegian mariners had discovered America some 1,000 years ago ... But neither Professor Holmboe, of Stockholm, nor the American archaeologists, have guessed the right age of the mounds, or the tumuli. The fact [is] that the Norwegians may have rediscovered the land that their long-forgotten forefathers believed to have perished in the general submersion [of Atlantis] ...'

Most occultists see the American Votan, and his prototype Wotan, as initiates – that is to say, as possessed of a perfect knowledge of the higher spiritual world hidden to ordinary men. This, they say, is confirmed in the traditional description of Votan as 'a son of the snake', which is one of the secret names for a person who has been initiated. The snake of occultism is the arch symbol of wisdom. It was wisdom which the snake encouraged Eve to take from the forbidden tree in Eden, just as the man-snake Votan gave the wisdom of writing to his own people. An early image of the Scandinavian hero Wotan riding his eight-legged horse Sleipnir shows a snake curled between the horse's many feet. In this a symbolic reference to the occult tradition of the serpent-man who is an initiate or magician?

It is a basic tenet of occult lore that writing was originally a magical art, the secrets of which were known only to initiates who eventually deemed that some of its secrets should be revealed to Man. Votan's knowledge of the art of writing in those prehistoric ages reminds us of the Scandinavian tradition that Wotan, the later name of Odin, was the father of poetry and inventor of the mysterious runic alphabet. This notion is reflected in the work of Gordon Wain, whose dramatic image of Odin, with his mystical hammer (itself a rune-symbol), incorporates two lines of runes upon the God's chariot.

Who was this Odin of Scandinavian mythology, and what are his secret runes? There are many different versions of the Nordic mythis, but we learn from some of them that Odin was the elder son of Thor, himself perpetually at war with the ancient giants (the *Jotunn*). Perhaps these were the same giants who, the occultists claim, lived on the continent which preceded that of Atlantis, and who survived in sufficient numbers into that culture to be troublesome to the Atlanteans. Odin too was a warrior, indeed he was adopted in later times as the hero of all warriors; yet at the same time he was a god of the dead, the giver of the art of poetry, and of the raven clan. The spread of the raven symbol throughout Europe was so extensive that it still figures in many coats of arms, and is usually an indication of early Scandinavian influences in the areas where it is found. Even the famous ravens which dwell with such dignity in that most ancient of all mystical sites in London, the Tower, are linked with the magical history of Odin, for he learned his secrets of the past and future from these birds. It is no accident that one of the names given in the Mithraic rites to a certain level of initiation was 'the raven'.

In the occult interpretation of the Norse legends we find Odin as the most important of the gods. The Ases, who were the rulers of the world which preceded our own, created the earth, the seas, the sky, the clouds and the whole visible realm from the physical remains of the slain giant Ymir: his flesh became the land, his blood the sea, his bones the mountains and his hair the trees. His enormous skull was raised on four pillars and turned into the vault of heaven, and the sparks of the fire kingdom of Juspellsheim became the stars and planets. However, the Ases did not have the power to create Man, and while they did mould his form from the inert and liveless trunks of two ash-trees, it was left to the magician Odin to breathe life into this wood after Lodur had turned it into blood and bones. In a word, it was Odin who gave Mankind its sense of identity and consciousness. The man so made was called Ask, and his female companion was called Embla: these were the pagan Adam and Eve of the ancient mythology. (The 'tree of life', magically transformed by Odin, also figures in the myths of the Hebraic Sephirothic Tree, the Norse Yggdrasil, the Hindu Aswatha and even in the Christian trees of Eden.) After granting Man life, Odin then gave him the supreme gifts of writing and literature.

Odin's invention of the secret letters we now call runes is said to have taken place after he hung for nine days on a gallows tree, and after he had agreed to pledge one of his eyes to the giant guardian of wisdom, Mimir. Mimir is one of the main characters of the Nordic myth *Volundar Kvida*, and this story is illustrated on the ancient rock of Externsteine. The occultists regard this sacrificed eye of Odin as the magical 'third eye', originally found at the root of the nose, which permitted Man direct vision of the

A dramatic image of Odin in his chariot, brandishing his magical hammer. After a painting by Gordon Wain. The artist has recorded some Scandinavian runes on the chariot to indicate that this nordic god was the inventor of both poetry and the magical system of runes.

spiritual world. It was the same as the secret eye of Horus, which survives as the *udjat* symbol, and it is the third eye found in the foreheads of many oriental images portraying the magical and invisible inner Man. Those who attempt to develop this third eye merely seek a way to perceive again the spiritual realms presently hidden from Man. Perhaps Odin's sacrifice recalls Man's loss of the third eye. Perhaps Man so keenly felt this loss of the higher world that he afterwards strove to develop a new relationship to the hidden spiritual heights by means of a magical alphabet. This is possible, for the ancient runes were sometimes called the language of the gods, and one of the later secret alphabets was named 'the writing of the angels'. It was by means of sacred writing that the priest communicated with the gods.

THE 'SECRET ART' OF RUNES

What is the nature of this strange 'secret art' of Odin, the Scandinavian alphabet which figures in mythology and magic and is found on many ancient stones and parchments? The word rune is derived from the Gothic *runa*, meaning secret, a word which passed into Anglo-Saxon as meaning secret whispering and is linked with the High German *raunen* which means to whisper. The runes are a collection of alphabetical letter forms which were supposed to have been used originally by the priests of the old Scandinavian mysteries, and which have survived carved on a wide variety of stones, bones and metalwork. A number of runes have also been found on old parchments, but most of these are medieval, rarely older than the twelfth century and almost certainly copied from earlier examples which are now lost.

From very early times, when the runes were first noted by European scholars, they were regarded as being a secret language and it was held that each of the letters incorporated magical principles. However, there is also evidence to show that runes were used for ordinary writing: according to Snorri, the author of the *Heimskringla* (circa AD 1100), the first man to use such runes to write down both old and new stories was Ari hin Frodi. The oldest known inscription in the early Nordic rune style is on a magical fibula from Stranda in Norway, and dates from about AD 800. (Some other runic styles are much older.) The transcription of the fibula rune, given by the historian Hans Jensen, reads 'The ornament is a protection against distress' – in other words, the runes turn the fibula into a magical amulet.

A stone built into the foundations of Gottorp castle, near Schleswig, and now in Kiel, appears to have been erected in AD 950 by Queen Asfrith, wife of King Knuba of Sweden, in memory of her son. It consists only of vertical runes, but other stones show runes alongside abstract patterns or even incised drawings, for example the Jelling Stones. Located near the Danish town of Vejle, the largest of these stones is a memorial erected by King Harald in the eleventh century, and is interestingly decorated at the top with abstract, curvilinear designs.

While runes are now recorded as letter-forms, originally the names of the individual runes were chosen so that the name reflected their sound. According to the ancient wisdom, sound was more important than written form, and all magic was conducted by means of sound or speech. This notion is reflected in many modern words, for example in the English word charm which came from the Latin *carmen* meaning song. The magical *sounds* were nowhere more intimately woven into the magical *forms* of the runes than in the recitation of runic poems, and these had a profound influence on Anglo-Saxon verse. Alongside the spoken and written runes was a system of magical writing which used graphic forms now called sigils. The most famous system of secret writing linked with runes is an inscription on a Swedish stone at Rök. It dates from the ninth century AD and included a series of what are called tent

A group of magicians using rune staves for magical purposes. A woodcut print of the sixteenth century, presumably derived from an illustration by Olaus Magnus. It is not clear what the magicians are doing, though magic of some sort is hinted at by the presence of the cosmic bodies of Moon (upper left) and Sun (upper right).

A huge boulder, inscribed with
banderoles of runes and interlacing
patterns, in the Ashmolean
Museum, Oxford.

runes (*tjaldrunir*), which are to be read in a clockwise direction. It is a memorial stone of
a magical nature, and is one of the longest ancient pagan runic inscriptions to have
survived.

Runes, and their various sigil derivatives, were used on rings, spearheads, and
other weapons with the idea of protecting the owner, or of investing him with more
power or skill in battle. An ancient gold ring, lost since World War I but known from
reproductions and copies, reads 'Property of the Goths. I am inviolable'. The promise of
safety in this inscription is sometimes interpreted as relating to the ring, and is viewed
as a magical recipe to avert theft, but it could also be seen as a magical charm to render
the *wearer* inviolable. The famous Björkertorp Stone, in Sweden, contains a runic
inscription which threatens death to anyone who dates disturb the monument. On the
arch above the eighteenth-century door of the church at Wieden (Oberpfalz), we find
the rune *Odal* which is supposed to give protection to the building. In the brickwork of
a house in Heide, in Germany, we find the *Man* rune, which is claimed to have a similar
protective power.

In the most impressive chambered megalithic tomb in Europe, at Maeshowe, in
Orkney, there are some runic inscriptions left by treasure-hunting Vikings in the
twelfth century, when they broke into the burial chamber. Among these runes is a
record of a Crusade made to the Holy Land, perhaps a reference to the fact that in 1151 a
number of men from Orkney went on this arduous fighting-trip to Jerusalem. The
Vikings who left these inscriptions were probably from Urnes in Norway, for among

Drawing of the eleventh-century rune-stone from Tjangvide, on the Swedish island of Gotland. The runes may be seen on the vertical banderoles to the top left and bottom right. The curious eight-legged horse is Sleipnir, the favourite mount of the god Odin, and the scene in the upper register of the stone has been interpreted as a representation of Odin being welcomed into Valhalla.

their magical letter forms they left behind a carving of a small dragon, which has been shown to relate to the carvings on the ancient church there.

Runes are found on some of the most interesting of all the ancient stones of Scandinavian countries. The largest Jelling Stone, which marks the conversion of the Danish King to Christianity in AD 965 combines pagan and Christian images with the runes. The image of Christ is swathed in a sea of interlaced patterns which are magical in origin, the swirl of lines being a symbol of the higher spiritual realm in which he lives. The carved funerary stone of Tjangvide on the Island of Gotland, in Sweden, is almost entirely magical in nature, and the runes on it are reduced almost to a minimum. The figure on horseback is Odin, and the ship below is probably the ship which carries the dead to the Underworld.

The forms of the ancient runes were probably derived from elementary sigils, or secret signs, as are the complex characters of the Chinese language. Because of this we should not be surprised to find that before the rune emerged into history (though they might already have been used secretly by priests along the lines proposed by Guido von List – see page 73), there was a developed system of magical symbols employed in Scandinavian countries. Striking examples are found among picture-stones on the Island of Gotland, and among these one of the most intriguing is that which shows two men holding shields, and two fabulous beasts, grouped around a decorative spiral motif.

The interpretation of this fifth-century limestone figure is no longer certain, but there are sufficient similarities to later medieval images for us to assume that the smaller circles around the quadriform spiral represent the five planets known to the pagan

STONES AND MAGIC SYMBOLS

The front panel of the Franks' Casket (British Museum, London). Runes frame a picture which has been linked with the pagan god Odin. The animal-headed figure to the extreme left is taken directly from the mystery wisdom imagery which was later adopted into the repertoire of European magic.

world. The one at the top is probably Saturn, that at the bottom Mercury, the one to the left Mars, and that to the right Venus. The designs on the shields almost certainly represent the Sun (left) and the Moon (right), which completes the septenary of 'planets'. The quadriform spiral may well represent the four phases of the lunar cycle during a period of one month – it is a device found on many carvings throughout northern Europe. Circular carvings similar to those in the smaller roundels are found in places as remote as the zodiacal doorway of San Michele in Susa (Italy), and are planetary images. Similarly, it is fascinating to note the similarity between the Venus symbol and depictions of the Star of Bethlehem on the seventh century Franks Casket (between the Madonna's head and the runic inscription to the right). It is characteristic of Nordic art of the period that the Christian imagery of the three Wise Men should appear in the same work as a Nordic myth telling how Wayland the Smith received Bodvild and her servant. Both images are surrounded by a border of magical runes.

We have seen then that Odin, being an initiate and magician, bequeathed to the Nordic races a pictorial alphabet charged with magical power. No wonder that when the Romans first encountered the Scandinavian mythology, they saw Odin as the equivalent of their planetary god Mercury, for Mercury was the one who introduced writing to men and who acted as the intermediary between the world of Man and the realms of Heaven and Hell. The wings on Mercury's feet, and even on his head in early images, carried him into the higher realm of the gods, while his magical staff (the *caduceus*) protected him from the demons of the infernal world, where he had to lead the newly-departed souls of men and women. In place of wings, Odin had his horse Sleipnir, and in place of a staff he had his drinking vessel. Is the ancient image of Mercury, which shows him holding snakes (derived from the form of his magical wand) yet another link with the snake that curls beneath Odin in the Tjangvide stone?

Wotan was clearly a representative of the white magicians of the Atlantean civilisation. Do we find any traces of the black magicians in the Scandinavian myths? Some of these stories tell us that Loki was one of the brothers of Odin, or, in the beginning, at least, one of his boon companions. The name Loki, we learn from such occultists as Blavatsky, is from the word *leichan*, meaning to enlighten. Loki is the 'dark brother' of the light Odin, for he became a black magician associated with the subterranean dwarfs while his 'light brother' was associated with the realm of Man. The ancient traditions relate that Atlantis fell victim to magical warfare conducted between the white and dark magicians, and this tradition may be hinted at in these mythological details. The most awful of Loki's offspring was Fenrir, who fathered a brood of wolves, obvious symbols of degeneration, in the north. With the coming of this brood, the power of the ancient gods diminished. It was one of these fearsome creatures, which we see in a demonic scroll of runes, who swallowed Odin at the titanic battle between the gods and giants. Is this terrible wolf a symbol of the end of the civilization which the great Atlantis once offered the world? Is it a herald of the dark period of chaos which separated that ancient history from the beginning of our own?

THE CURIOUS HISTORY OF THE SWASTIKA

This theme of darkness reminds us that the swastika has had a curious history in regard to the runes – mainly as a result of certain pseudo-occult claims made about it in the early part of this century by German Nationalists. We have already noted (page 73) how von Liebensfels raised a flag bearing the swastika over what he designated as a 'Templar castle' at Burg Wurfenstein in 1907. In fact this was certainly not the first use of the symbol for German nationalistic purposes. The founder of the occultist section of the German Nationalists, Guido von List, had supposed the original Germanic race to have been headed by a priestly cast of initiates called the *Armanen*, of the Hermiones tribe. Von List's interest in occult lore, and its relation to the romance-history of the Teutonic tribes, appears to have come to a mystical head after an operation on his eyes in 1902 which left him blind for several months. It was during this period that the 'mysteries' of the runes were revealed to him, and he was permitted insights into the esoteric history of the Aryans. Needless to say, von List's insights into the history of such symbols was based largely upon his own imagination and derived from his supposed clairvoyant perception, yet in spite of this his views, as revealed in the nationalist folklore of his books *German Mythological Landscapes* and *The Secret of the Runes*, did have a considerable influence towards the end of the last century.

Von List had maintained that one of the holy symbols of the *Armanen* was the runic swastika, which he called the *fyrfos*, and for this reason he traced its form in the most unlikely places and designs in order to show that many of the standard Christian, heraldic and mythological symbols were derived from the ancient wisdom of Nordic tribes. His view of the runes was intensely personal, and he traced runic devices as 'secret structures' in almost every symbol imaginable. For example, the Maltese Cross (which was essentially a purely Christian symbol) was, according to von List's view of things, nothing more than a 'secret *fyrfos*', since the left-hand side and short descending declivity of each of the four arms of the cross marked out the runic symbol. In particular, the *fyrfos* rune interested him as a particularly meaningful symbol of the triune world, and he used it in certain of his own rites practised by the pseudo-occult Armanen group. He left an account of one rite in which he, as one of the survivors of the original Armanen group, used the runic swastika in a bizarre expedition. At the summer solstice in 1875, he and a group of like-minded friends trekked to the hilltop site of the ancient Roman city of Carnuntum (near Vienna) and ritually lit a fire. Later, they buried in its embers eight wine bottles, arranged in the pattern of a swastika. Little did they know that they were planting dragon-seeds which would sprout vast armies.

The association between German armies and the mysticism of von List led to a particularly important prediction which fuelled the Nazi's feelings of superiority even during the early years of the movement. Von List had made a prophecy, based on a term from a translation of the Old Norse *Edda*, which might have been a reference to Christ Himself but which he de-Christianised and termed *der Starke von Oben* (the Strong One from Above). For some time this was interpreted as relating to a leader, or *Fuhrer*. Towards the end of World War I, von List reinterpreted the term to mean that the spirits of those Germans killed in battle would be reincarnated and, in the year 1932, would once again involved themselves in a Germanic struggle. In passing, however, we should observe that von List's understanding of reincarnation was as far removed from the esoteric tradition as was his interpretation of the runes: no reliable occult tradition suggests that human beings are reincarnated immediately after their deaths.

Curiously enough, the connection between the summer solstice and the runic swastika, which von List had popularised in his writings, is still preserved in the eyrie-like chapel near the top of a pinnacle in that strange stronghold of Germanic sentiment, the Externsteine. Someone, presumably during the period of Nazi ascendancy, carved the swastika deep into the primitive stone altar of this chapel. Now, the interesting thing is that this altar, which is of a very primitive style and is clearly very ancient, stands below a porthole which has been so designed to allow the beams of the newly-rising sun to fall directly through the length of the chapel and centre upon the alcove behind. The picture of the chapel on page 113 clearly shows the design of the chapel, with the porthole wall to the right, the alcove to the left, and the well-risen sun projecting its circle onto the wall behind. This picture was taken about two hours after

LEONJINPACI

A Christian swastika from a tomb in the Roman catacombs. It is moving in the opposite direction to the apparent movement of the Sun. The curious gesture of the man (presumably Leo, or Leon), who has his arms raised, with palms outwards, follows a convention of early Christian art which was derived from Egyptian sacred writing. In Egyptian hieroglyphics a pair of raised arms (with palms open to the viewer) represented the ka-spirit of the deceased. The Christians adopted this symbolic form to indicate that the person depicted is actually in ka-form, or spirit form, which is to say it is a portrayal of someone who is dead in the physical sense, but alive in the spiritual realm.

sunrise, exactly one month before the solstice. A person who considered the swastika to be linked with solar symbolism, and especially with the solstice period, might be forgiven the sacrilege of carving the figure on the top of the altar.

In spite of the historical evidence, von List and Liebensfels (who was to some extent influenced by him) proclaimed that the swastika had been derived from German runes, and this idea, along with other nationalistically-orientated notions set out in his books, had a great influence on occult thought in Germany. However, both men were sufficient scholars to recognise that the anti-clockwise swastika had been used as a Buddhist symbol for well over 2,000 years as an amulet of good fortune, and had been adopted by certain European esoteric societies as a beneficient symbol. Even in their beloved Nordic countries, the swastika had been used as early as the Iron Age, as evidenced by the bronze-work decorations on four-wheeled chariots found in a bog at Dejbjerg, in Jutland. The several swastikas found here are somewhat reminiscent of the ancient symbol carved on the Swastika Stone above Ilkley, in Yorkshire.

The anti-clockwise swastika had a similar antiquity in ancient Greece, where it was used on coins from Syracuse (then a Greek colony) which may be dated to the fourth century BC. An image of such a swastika is still preserved among the mosaics from the second-century Roman settlement at Paphos, in Cyprus. When Hitler (partly following the arguments of Dr. Friedrich Krohn, and no doubt influenced by the writings of both Liebenfels and von List) adopted the swastika as the National Socialist emblem, it was undoubtedly for magical reasons. The swastika was already well established through the Volkisch literature as an anti-semitic symbol, and had appeared in several publications relating to the master race. Some German scholars had even done the impossible, and shown that the swastika was indeed derived from those magical runes supposed to have been the original written language of the Teutonic race. In making the profound, and entirely personal, decision to reverse the swastika for his emblem, Hitler probably considered that in so doing he was countering the spiritual work of the esoteric groups he so despised.

When Hitler finally adopted the swastika as the emblem for his newly-formed Nazi party in 1920, he was already persuaded (mainly through the writings of such seers as von List) that it was a pre-eminently Nordic symbol derived from Germanic runes. However, it was his personal decision to reverse the swastika design proposed by Dr. Friedrich Krohn, and so give it its distinctive anti-clockwise form. By this reversal, what had been intended as a life-giving emblem of good fortune and beneficence was turned inside out – perhaps for entirely magical reasons. It is quite possible that this decision arose from Hitler's wish to counter the widespread magical use of the swastika practised by such powerful esoteric groups as the Theosophists, who had incorporated the symbol into their own emblematic devices.

An instructive example of the Theosophical use of the swastika may be seen on the binding of the 1910 edition of Rudolf Steiner's *Initiation and Its Results* (English edition), first published in magazine form in Leipzig. Here the swastika follows the Buddhist tradition, and is emblematic (among other things) of good fortune, and of the solar movement in which all humans are bathed and from which they derive their inner life. The curious black symbols behind the encircled yellow swastika do not appear to

The title page of Rudolf Steiner's seminal book, *Initiation and its Results*, incorporates a logo which brings together a number of occult symbols, including the rosy-cross of the Rosicrucian movement, and the pentagram, or five-pointed star, which was an esoteric symbol in ancient Egypt.

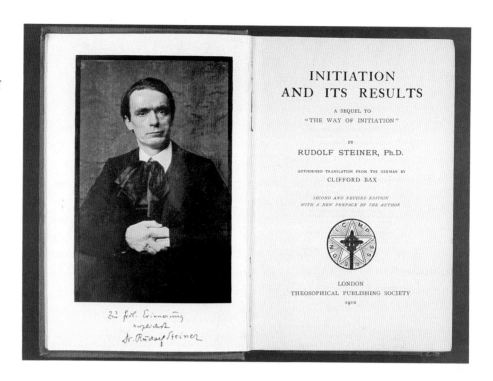

make much sense at first glance. However, a note beneath the colophon of the book informs us that the translator and editor of the Steiner text, faced with so many unauthorised translations of the 'Master's' work, had decided to adopt the pentagram and Rosy-Cross symbol in order to authenticate the book. Of course, what this note does *not* say (but what is probably of most importance) is that one consequence of this decision to incorporate the Rosy-Cross symbol was that it announced Steiner's affiliation to the Rosicrucian tradition – not something which had been part of the original Theosophical programme.

It has been widely recognised by occultists that other ancient runes were also adopted by the Nazis as part of the new Teutonic mythology which they sought to promote. Just as the Nazis adopted what was in effect an ancient solar symbol for their 'regeneration' swastika, they also took over a Nordic sigil to represent the aspirations of the SS. This was a sigil derived from the *sig* – the runic sound 'sig' being associated with the German *sieg*, meaning victory. The Nazi organisation for youth, *Deutsche Jungvolk*, adopted a single sig rune as its emblematic device, and the same symbol was adapted for their equivalent of the Christian-based Red Cross.

That extraordinary symbol of German unity at the Deutsches Eck, in Koblenz, the memorial originally designed for Wilhelm I, also contains some early symbols which, whilst not derived from the runes, were widely used in esoteric circles. Of particular interest is the use of the letter W, which might be assumed by the uninitiated to be a reference to the first letter of Wilhelm's name. However, the specific form was figured as two interlaced Vs, which means that it is intended to refer to the Greek-derived form *nike*, meaning victory. This sigil was used in pre-Christian times but is also found among early Christian symbols.

MODERN RUNE DIVINATION

In recent years the runes have gained much popularity as fortune-telling devices, yet there is little to suggest that these practices have anything to do with the true magic of runic divination. The Roman historian Tacitus left an account of how the Germans consulted the runes for the purpose of divination. Their method was to cut a bough from a fruit-bearing tree and then slice this into small pieces, after which each one was marked with a rune. These marked sticks were then thrown at random into a white cloth whilst the gods were invoked. The priest and the community (presumably the lay brethren) then took up from the cloth three sticks at random, one at a time, and interpreted their meanings according to the runes marked upon them.

Few modern practitioners of rune-reading will go to such lengths as these German priests, and most are more inclined to purchase their rune sticks already made and marked, designed specifically for divination. The systems used today essentially convert the runes into the equivalent of a pack of cards, to which are ascribed complex associations and meanings. The pattern of runes, no matter how it is attained, is read along the lines of the formal order of a Tarot pack or the hexagram of the Chinese *I Ching, The Book of Change*. The fact that there are many different rune systems in use today is confusing for the uninitiated, but perhaps the most useful system is that proposed by Werner Kosbab in *Das Runen-Orakel* (1982). He combines the modern 18 rune system with a few of the older forms, along with sigils derived from the hermetic tradition.

The rune-system proposed by the German writer Werner Kosbab. The 56 sigils are not all nordic runes, however. Among them (fourth line down, reading from right to left) we find the sigils for the planet Venus, for the astrological aspect of opposition, the sigils for Mars, Jupiter and Saturn, the sigils for the astrological aspects of Trine and Square, and a rune which is also a geomantic sigil. Artwork based on the figures in the 1982 edition of Kosbab's *Das Runene-Orakel*.

Bibliography

Agrippa, Henricus Cornelius *De Occult Philosophia,* in the K.A. Nowotny edition of 1967 (published Graz, Austria, 1967).

Anati, Emmanuel *Capo di Ponte,* Edizioni del Centro, Brescia, 1975.

Aspeslag, Pierre *Chapel of the Holy Blood, Bruges,* S. V. van Mieghem, Oostende, 1988.

Barber, Malcolm *The Trial of the Templars,* Cambridge, 1978.

Begg, Ean *The Cult of the Black Virgin,* RKP, Henley-on-Thames, 1985.

Blavatsky, H. P. *The Secret Doctrine: the Synthesis of Science, Religion and Philosophy,* The Pasadena (California) 1970 reprint of the 1888 edition.

Carlgren, Franz *Rudolf Steiner 1861–1927,* Dornach 1972.

Chailley, Jacques *The Magic Flute, Masonic Opera. An Interpretation of the Libretto and the Music,* translated from the French by Herbert Weinstock, Gollancz, London, 1972.

Charpentier, Josane *La Sorcellerie en Pays Basque,* Librairie Guenegaud, 1977.

Charpentier, Louis *Les Mystères Templiers,* Robert Laffont, Paris, 1967.

Charpentier, Louis *The Mysteries of Chartres Cathedral,* English translation by Ronald Fraser in collaboration with Janette Jackson, Thorsons, Northampton, 1972.

Crowley, Aleister *Magick in Theory and Practice by The Master Therion,* Castle Books, New York, n.d.

Donnelly, Ignatius *Atlantis – The Antediluvian World,* 1882.

Doumayrou, Guy-Rene *Evocations de l'Espirit des Lieux,* Beziers: Centre International de Documentation Occitane, 1987.

Fulcanelli *Fulcanelli: Master Alchemist. Le Mystère des Cathédrales. Esoteric interpretation of the Hermetic Symbols of the Great Work,* translated from the French by Mary Sworder, Neville Spearman, London, 1971.

Gettings, Fred *The Hidden Art,* Studio Vista, London, 1978.

Gettings, Fred *The Secret Zodiac,* RKP, Henley-on-Thames, 1987.

Guazzo, Francesco Maria *Compendium Maleficarum,* translated by A. E. Ashwin, with notes by Montague Summers, John Rodker, London, 1929.

Hawkins, G. S. *Stonehenge Decoded,* London 1965.

Jensen, Hans *Sign, Symbol and Script: an Account of Man's Efforts to Write,* translated from the German by George Unwin, Allen and Unwin, London, 1970.

Lévi Eliphas *Transcendental Magic. Its Doctrine and Ritual,* translated by A. E. Waite, John Story, Sheffield, 1896.

Lockyer, J. N. *Stonehenge and Other British Monuments Astronomically Considered,* revised edition, London, 1909. See also 'On Sun and Star Temples' in *Nature,* July 1891.

Michell, John *A Little History of Astro-archaeology. Stages in the Transformation of a Heresy,* Thames and Hudson, London, 1977.

Ouspensky, P. D. *A New Model of the Universe,* RKP, Henley-on-Thames, 2nd edition, 1934

Penrose, F. C. 'A Preliminary Statement on an Investigation of a Number of Greek Temples . . .' *Proceedings of the Royal Society,* April 1893.

Phaure, Jean *Introduction à la Géorgraphie Sacrée de Paris, Barque d'Isis,* Editions du Borrego, Paris, 1985.

Plancy, Collin de *Dictionnaire Infernale,* Edition Princeps Integrale. Bibliothèque Marabout, 1973.

Robbins, Rossell Hope *The Encyclopedia of Witchcraft and Demonology,* London and New York, 1959.

Psicon. *Rivista Internazionale di Architettura,* Ott-Dic 1974.

Runciman, Steven *The Medieval Manichee: A Study of the Christian Dualist Heresy,* Cambridge, 1969.

Sede, Gerard de *Rennes-le-Château. Le Dossier, Les Impostures, Les Phantasmes, Les Hypothèses,* R. Laffont, Paris, 1988.

Steiner, Rudolf *The Temple Legend: Freemasonry and Related Occult Movements,* English translation by J. M. Wood from notes unrevised by Steiner, from a series of twenty lectures given in German, in Berlin between 1904 and 1906.

Steiner, Rudolf *Initiation and its Results,* translated from the German by Clifford Bax, Theosophical Publishing Society, London, 1910.

Taylor, René 'Architecture and Magic: Considerations on the Idea of the Escorial', in *Essays in the History of Architecture Presented to Rudolf Wittkower,* edited by D. Fraser, H. Hibbard and M. J. Lewine, 1967.

Verardi M. Letizia Troccoli *I Misteriosi Simboli dei Trulli,* Editorale Adda, 1972.

Waite, Arthur Edward *The Real History of the Rosicrucians,* George Redway, London, 1887.

Watkins, A *The Old Straight Track,* London, 1925.

Wunderlich, Hans Georg *The Secret of Crete,* translated from the German by Richard Winston, Macmillan, London, 1974.

Yates, Frances A. *The Rosicrucian Enlightenment,* RKP, Henley-on-Thames, 1972.

Acknowledgements

With the exception of the picture on page 183, which is by courtesy of the Trustees of the British Museum, all the photographs were provided by Charles Walker and supplied thorough Images Colour Library Ltd., Leeds and London. The photographer would like to thank the following museums for kind permission to photograph the pictures on the following pages: National Museum, Lisbon, p. 19; Kunthistorische Museum, Vienna, p. 50; Musée Condé, Chantilly, p. 59; Ashmolean Museum, Oxford, p. 181. Several of the black and white pictures are printed from colour transparencies. Charles Walker would like to thank all those individuals who have helped him during his travels and researches throughout Europe.

Index